THE BAT SCIENTISTS

itse

By pulling in its wings
and braking with its tail,
his big brown bat slows
lf for landing.

THE BAT SCIENTISTS

Mary Kay Carson

with photographs by Tom Uhlman

sandpiper

Houghton Mifflin Harcourt

Boston   New York

Text copyright © 2010 by Mary Kay Carson
Photographs copyright © 2010 by Tom Uhlman with the exception of the following:
p. 11 (horseshoe and ghost bats), p. 17, and p. 36 (California leaf-nosed bat)—Merlin Tuttle
p. 16—Bat Conservation International
p. 68 (bottom right)—Photo courtesy of Ryan von Linden/New York Department of Environmental Conservation

SANDPIPER and the SANDPIPER logo are trademarks of Houghton Mifflin Harcourt Publishing Company.

For information about permission to reproduce selections from this book,
write to Permissions, Houghton Mifflin Harcourt Publishing Company,
215 Park Avenue South, New York, New York 10003.

www.hmhbooks.com
Design by Ellen Nygaard
The text of this book is set in Scala.
Maps by Rachel Newborn

The Library of Congress has cataloged the hardcover edition as follows:
Carson, Mary Kay.
The bat scientists / Mary Kay Carson ; with photographs by Tom Uhlman.
p. cm.
I. Bats—Research—Juvenile literature. 2. Mammalogists—Juvenile literature. I. Title.
QL737.C5C356 2010
599.4—dc22
2010006767

ISBN: 978-0-547-19956-6 hardcover
ISBN: 978-0-544-10493-8 paperback

Manufactured in China
SCP 10 9 8 7 6 5 4 3 2 1

4500415526

To those in the trenches against white-nose syndrome.
Good luck and Godspeed.

—M.K.C. and T.U.

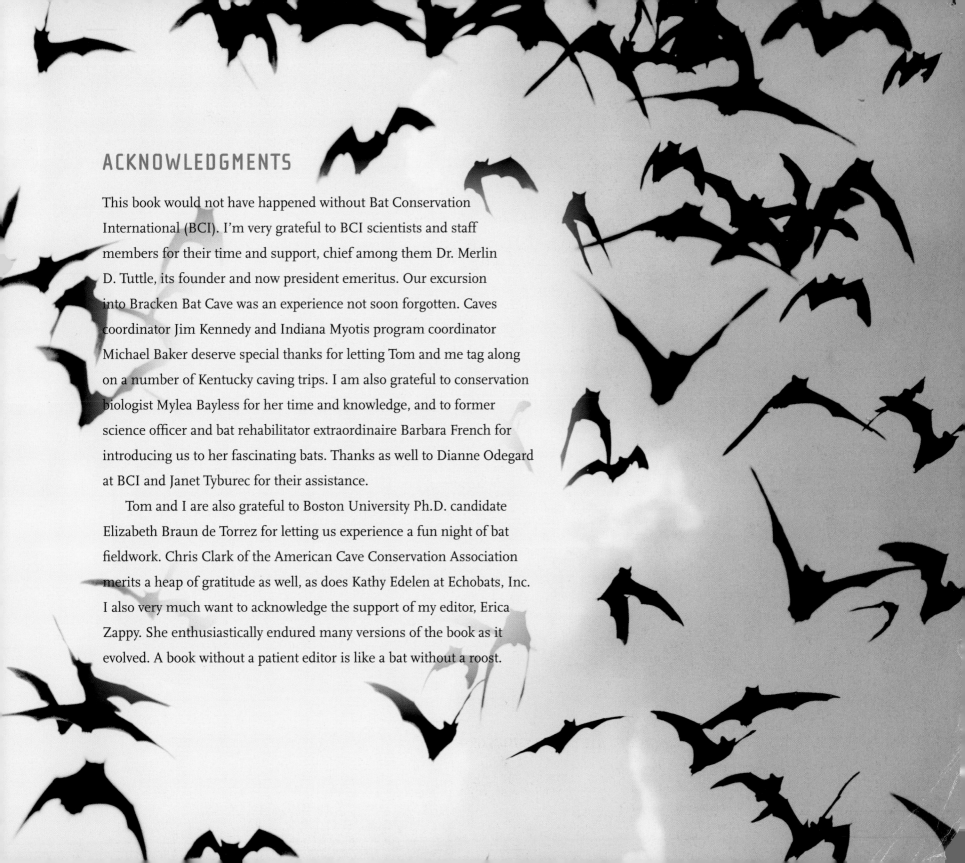

ACKNOWLEDGMENTS

This book would not have happened without Bat Conservation International (BCI). I'm very grateful to BCI scientists and staff members for their time and support, chief among them Dr. Merlin D. Tuttle, its founder and now president emeritus. Our excursion into Bracken Bat Cave was an experience not soon forgotten. Caves coordinator Jim Kennedy and Indiana Myotis program coordinator Michael Baker deserve special thanks for letting Tom and me tag along on a number of Kentucky caving trips. I am also grateful to conservation biologist Mylea Bayless for her time and knowledge, and to former science officer and bat rehabilitator extraordinaire Barbara French for introducing us to her fascinating bats. Thanks as well to Dianne Odegard at BCI and Janet Tyburec for their assistance.

Tom and I are also grateful to Boston University Ph.D. candidate Elizabeth Braun de Torrez for letting us experience a fun night of bat fieldwork. Chris Clark of the American Cave Conservation Association merits a heap of gratitude as well, as does Kathy Edelen at Echobats, Inc. I also very much want to acknowledge the support of my editor, Erica Zappy. She enthusiastically endured many versions of the book as it evolved. A book without a patient editor is like a bat without a roost.

CONTENTS

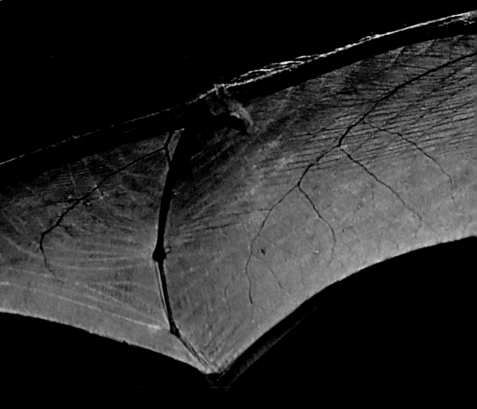

BAT BASICS 8

BAT BENEFITS 10

CHAPTER 1

WORKING IN THE DARK 13

BAT PREDATORS 21

CHAPTER 2

CHANGING MINDS, RESCUING BATS 27

BATTY MYTHS 38

CHAPTER 3

GOING UNDERGROUND 41

HOW A CAVE TRAPS COLD AIR 45

GATING LAUREL CAVE 48

CHAPTER 4

BUILDING BAT HOMES 53

CELEBRITY BRIDGE BATS 60

MINES FOR BATS 64

CHAPTER 5

DISCOVERING BATS' SECRETS 67

ENSURING SURVIVAL 71

KILLER WIND 74

LEARN MORE ABOUT BATS 78

WORDS TO KNOW 79

INDEX 80

A big brown bat finds its way in the dark by calling out as it flies.

BAT BASICS

WHAT? Bats are mammals that have wings and fly.

WHERE? Bats live on every continent except Antarctica.

WHEN? Bats are nocturnal, or active at night. They sleep during the day, hanging upside down in a roost.

HOW MANY? There are about 1,100 species of bats.

BIGGEST BAT? A flying fox can weigh more than 3 pounds (1.5 kilograms) and have a wingspan of up to 6 feet (1.8 meters).

SMALLEST BAT? A bumblebee bat weighs less than a penny (2 grams) with a wingspan of only 6.5 inches (17 centimeters).

LIFE SPAN? Bats are long lived for their size—some have lived more than forty years.

BAT BABIES? Most bats have a single pup per year, though some kinds have twins or triplets.

FOOD? Many bats are insect-eaters, but there are also bats that eat fruit, nectar, fish, frogs, birds, or blood.

DANGEROUS? Bats are timid creatures that generally avoid people.

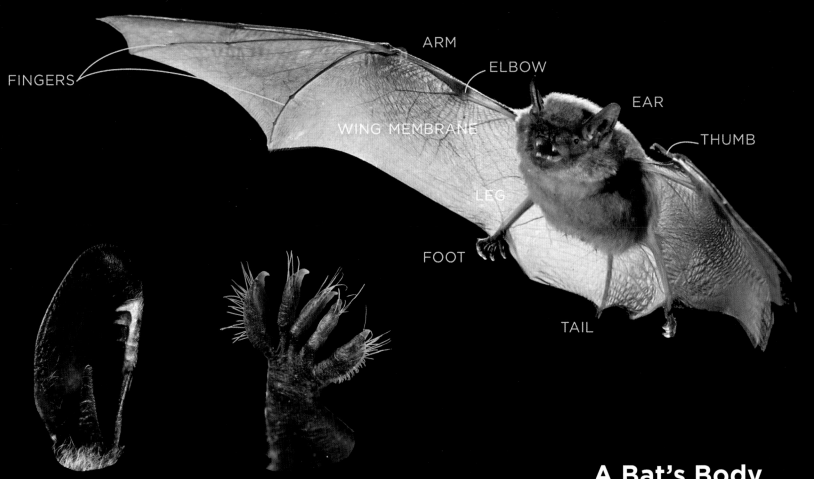

FINGERS

ARM

ELBOW

WING MEMBRANE

EAR

THUMB

LEG

FOOT

TAIL

EAR CLOSE-UP

FOOT CLOSE-UP

A Bat's Body

A bat's body is adapted to its airborne lifestyle. Its flexible wings are made up of arm and hand bones covered in a thin, hairless membrane of skin. The feet lock into a clamped position when the bat's asleep so it can hang from its roost while resting. And a bat's large ears help it hear the echoed sounds it bounces off prey and obstacles in flight.

BAT BENEFITS

Bats are amazing creatures that play important roles in their ecosystems. People around the world also directly benefit from bats in many ways, including these:

BUG CONTROL. Bats eat enormous numbers of night-flying insects, including crop, garden, and disease-carrying pests. One little brown bat can catch 1,000 mosquito-size insects in a single hour!

FOOD FOR PEOPLE. Fruit- and nectar-eating bats pollinate many flowers and spread the seeds of trees, plants, and shrubs. Many of these plants provide important foods, including bananas, mangos, cashews, dates, figs, breadfruit, saguaro, and agave.

FOREST REGROWTH. Rainforest and other tropical bats are essential carriers of seeds that help regrow cut or burned forests.

INVENTION INSPIRATION. A chemical in vampire bat spit that breaks up blood clots helped scientists develop a new treatment for people who've had strokes. Studying how bats echolocate inspired a new kind of cane for the blind that uses bounced sound to help its user get around safely.

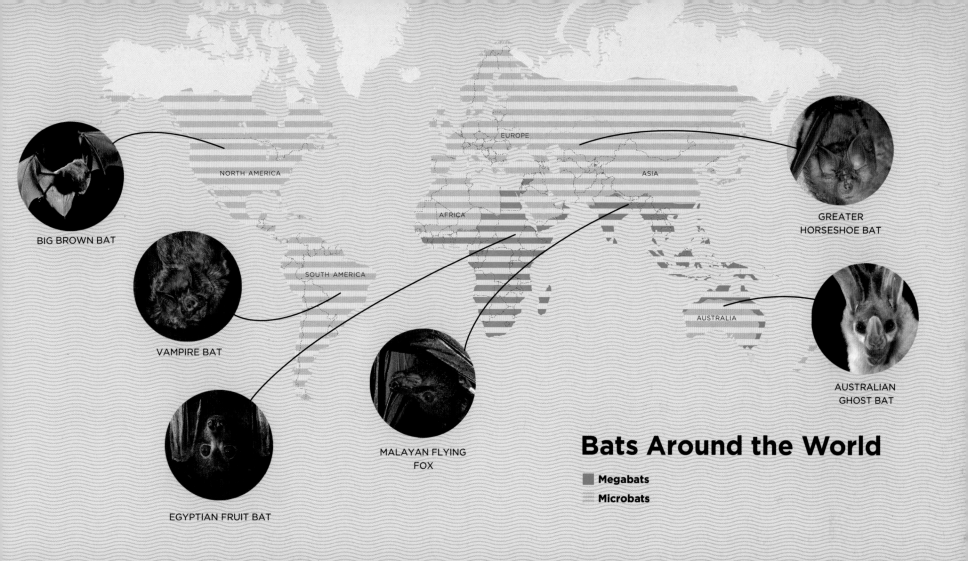

BIG BROWN BAT

NORTH AMERICA

EUROPE

ASIA

AFRICA

GREATER
HORSESHOE BAT

SOUTH AMERICA

VAMPIRE BAT

AUSTRALIA

AUSTRALIAN
GHOST BAT

MALAYAN FLYING
FOX

EGYPTIAN FRUIT BAT

Bats Around the World

■ **Megabats**
▬ **Microbats**

Bats live everywhere except the coldest ends of the earth. Bats are divided into two main groups: megachiroptera (megabats) and microchiroptera (microbats). Megabats are large-to-medium-size bats with large eyes, which live in Africa, Asia, and Australia. The 170 species of megabats are also sometimes called Old World fruit bats because of their diet, or flying foxes because of their foxlike faces. Microbats make up most of the bat species and live around the world. Microbats are small-to-medium-size bats with small eyes; they mostly eat insects, though some eat fruit, nectar, blood, or fish.

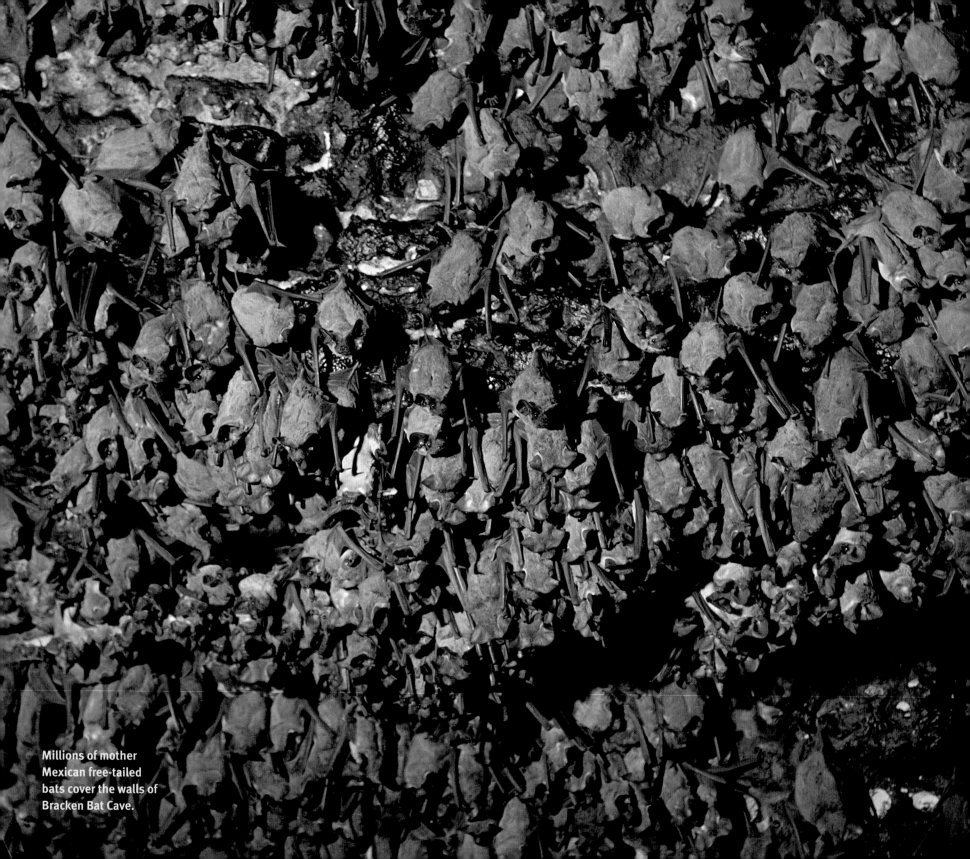

Millions of mother Mexican free-tailed bats cover the walls of Bracken Bat Cave.

CHAPTER 1

WORKING IN THE DARK

"Do you see them?" asks a muffled voice. A mask covers Merlin Tuttle's mouth, mustache, and nose, and it makes the bat scientist hard to understand. He also wears a hardhat with a headlamp and carries a big flashlight. The flashlight lights up small circles of wriggling bats on the cave walls. Bats are everywhere inside the soccer-arena-size cave. Millions of identical-looking bats hang from the rock walls and ceiling. A few fly around, circling overhead. Each bat is small, grayish brown, and furry, with wings of smooth, silky skin. All have big ears, bright black eyes, and a skinny tail that sticks out between the legs. They are Mexican free-tailed bats. Twenty million of them make Bracken Bat Cave near San Antonio, Texas, their summer home. It's the largest known colony of bats in the world.

Bat scientist Merlin Tuttle examines a bat in Bracken Bat Cave. You can see the Mexican free-tailed bat's tail hanging down between its legs, which earns it its name. Most bat tails are covered in wing membrane.

Mexican free-tailed bat babies, called pups, are born hairless.

live young nursed with milk. But bats are unlike any other kind of mammal in an extraordinary way. Bats can fly.

HOME HARSH HOME

About 270 tons of bats crowd inside Bracken Bat Cave during the summer. That's the body weight of more than fifty elephants! All those bats really heat the cave up. Temperatures reach well over a humid 100°F (38°C). Sweat soaks Merlin's shirt as he attaches a camera to a tripod. The mask only makes him feel hotter, but it's necessary. The respirator mask keeps the bat scientist from breathing in ammonia gas. "Ammonia will burn your lungs, throat, and nose," warns Merlin. It's the same strong-smelling chemical in window cleaner. The ammonia in the cave starts with what 20 million pooping and peeing bats create. Bat droppings continually rain down inside the cave. The dark rice-shaped droppings, called guano, pile up on the cave floor.

Merlin wears tall rubber boots to walk over the giant mounds of guano. His feet sink in with each step, leaving deep footprints. But the footprints don't last. The guano-covered ground is moving! Millions of beetles squirm in the bat droppings. Their movements quickly blur the footprints as they eat and churn the guano into piles of brownish dust.

"There are some pups," says Merlin, pointing his light upward. He speaks loudly to be heard through the mask and over the chattering bats. On a wall of squashed-together squirming bats are some pinkish spots. A closer look reveals furless, pink-skinned, newborn baby bats—the pups Merlin was pointing to. Bracken Cave is a maternity colony. All of the adult bats there are females. "Each mother gives birth to a single pup once a year," explains Merlin. Bats are mammals, like dogs, tigers, and people. They are furred animals that give birth to

These beetles are the real cause of the cave's dangerous ammonia gas, pumping it out as a waste product as they feed on guano. The beetles are also flesh eaters that prey on fallen, dying, or dead bats. A pup that loses its grip and falls to the floor is doomed. Before it can crawl back up the cave wall, beetles swarm it. "An hour later it's a skeleton," says Merlin. Bat bones litter the cave floor as proof.

Bracken Bat Cave is a harsh environment, but it suits the bats. The high temperatures keep the pups warm while the mothers leave at night to catch insects. Like all bats, Mexican free-tails are nocturnal. They sleep during the day and hunt at night. The cave's rough, rocky walls are perfect for pup feet to grip. Even the ammonia gas works for the bats: it helps keep out some predators. Merlin doesn't seem to mind the constant rain of poop, pee, and tiny blood-sucking bat mites falling down from overhead. He concentrates on taking a picture of the bat-covered walls. Merlin will use the picture to help estimate how many bats are in the cave. About two hundred adult bats will roost within a single square foot of cave wall. As many as five hundred pups can squeeze into that same space. "I want to compare the picture with one I shot twenty years ago," he says as he wipes a bat dropping off his camera. Merlin has visited amazing wildlife sites all over the world, but Bracken Bat Cave is his favorite.

FROM NATURE BOY TO BATMAN

Merlin Tuttle can't remember a time when nature didn't fascinate him. Even as a little kid he collected seashells, brought home toads, and kept a journal of his wildlife observations. "I happened to get especially interested in bats beginning when I was about nine," says Merlin. He came across some bats living in an old cabin. That started him researching and reading about bats. When Merlin was a teenager, his family moved to Tennessee. Their new home just happened to be near a bat cave. "I caught some and identified them in a book," remembers Merlin. They were gray bats. "The book said that this was a species that lived in the same cave year round and didn't migrate." After a year of watching when the bats entered and exited the cave, Merlin figured out that the books were wrong. These gray bats weren't there all year—they migrated.

Armed with what he'd learned, high school kid Merlin Tuttle convinced scientists at the Smithsonian Institution that they might be wrong. "They gave me several thousand bat bands and said, 'Why don't you go back and band them and see if you can figure out where they go,'" remembers Merlin. Bat bands are small metal clips with identification numbers on them. The bands fit around a bat's winged arm like a bracelet. Merlin Tuttle ended up studying gray bats for many years. He

Merlin photographs bats inside Bracken Bat Cave.

Merlin estimates the numbers of endangered gray bats hibernating in Tennessee's Pearson's Cave. Thanks to decades of work, gray bat numbers have greatly increased. Unfortunately the species is now threatened by white-nose syndrome.

FACING PAGE: Merlin took this stunning photograph of an amazing lesser long-nosed bat. It is eating the nectar and pollen of a giant saguaro cactus flower.

visited their caves all across the southeastern United States through college and after he became a bat scientist. "I eventually banded over forty thousand bats and traced some of the migrants all the way from Florida to the Virginia border," says Merlin. Because of his research, books had to be rewritten to say that gray bats not only migrate, but also often travel a really long way.

FROM SCIENTIST TO CONSERVATIONIST

Merlin kept studying bats and other animals through college. He eventually got an advanced degree in mammalogy, the study of mammals, the kind of animals bats are. While Merlin became a respected bat scientist in the 1970s, bats themselves got very little respect. Merlin traveled around the world studying bats—Africa, Asia, Latin America, and North America. "Everywhere I went, people were killing bats in large numbers just out of ignorance," says Merlin. Many people are afraid of bats. Bats live in dark spooky places like caves and abandoned buildings, and only come out at night. Merlin saw bat caves dynamited or bulldozed shut. Misguided farmers told him they killed bats to protect their fruit trees or crops. Even the caves where Merlin studied gray bats were under attack. In 1976 Merlin visited an Alabama cave that was once home to 250,000 gray bats. What he found shocked

him. All the bats were gone. Inside the cave were sticks, stones, rifle cartridges, and fireworks wrappers.

Merlin Tuttle decided he had to do something to help the bats he loved to study, so he started an organization in 1982. It wasn't easy. "When I started Bat Conservation International (BCI), most people would've rather paid to kill a bat than to save one," says Merlin. "They ranked between cockroaches and rattlesnakes in opinion polls." People misunderstand bats. They mistakenly believe that bats are blind, fierce, disease-carrying, scary critters that want to bite. So Merlin set out to educate people about how gentle, amazing, and important bats really are.

Photography quickly became an important tool. "People fear most what they understand least," explains Merlin. Bats are misunderstood partly because they are hard to see. Bats fly at night and spend the day in dark places. When Merlin started writing books about bats, most photographs showed bats with snarling teeth held up by their wings. Merlin knew the bats in the photographs looked frightening because they were scared and stressed. So he started taking his own photographs of bats at ease—bats just being bats. His stunning natural photos soon showed up in magazines and books. The photos of bats flying, eating nectar, catching fish, and caring for pups helped people see bats for what they really are—and want to save them.

The large, wide entrance to Bracken Bat Cave is part of what makes it such a great place for a maternity colony.

WATCHING OUT FOR BATS

The baking-hot summer sun is finally low in the sky at Bracken Bat Cave. Merlin Tuttle has packed up his camera and trudged back over the guano mounds. There's no sign of his earlier footprints—the beetles already erased them. Once out of the sweltering cave, he sits on a bench to clean the bat mites out of his hair. But his day is far from over.

Bats are gathering just inside the oval-shaped cave entrance. They chatter and fly laps around the entrance, their thousands of beating bat wings making a windy sound. A whiff of ammonia drifts on the breeze. And then the bats start flowing out. They seem to move as one, like a cloud of thick, chunky smoke streaming out of the cave's entrance for hours. It's hard to pick out individual bats, there are so many. The bats spiral up and up like a tightly wound tornado column. Then they head away from the cave in a ribbon of bats that stretches to the horizon.

Bracken Bat Cave's Mexican free-tailed bats are bound for area farm fields. Some may travel one hundred miles (160 km) away. The hungry moms will feed on crop pests, such as corn earworm moths. "They eat about two hundred tons of insects every summer night," says Merlin. In the early morning, the moms will return to nurse their pups. Not all of them will make it back. Predators also know when the bats come out. Hawks and owls dive-bomb them, snagging bats with their dagger-like talons. Snakes lie in wait among the rocks. They wait for a sudden gust of wind to push an unlucky bat to the ground as it exits the cave. When it happens, a long coachwhip snake will strike, clamping its jaws around the bat's body and leaving its wings to beat outside its closed mouth. Bats eat, and they are eaten. They are part of the ecosystem of the cave, the surrounding scrub, and the farmlands. Watching them in action is something to remember.

Merlin photographs bats streaming out of Bracken Bat Cave (left), and bats inside the cave (right).

A coachwhip snake gets a meal, but one bat pup's mother will not be returning to the roost tonight.

Predators like domestic cats and raccoons (top) hunt bats from the ground, while great horned owls and barred owls (middle) catch them in the air. Mexican free-tailed bats are the prey of this Swainson's hawk (bottom left). Camouflaged coloring helps many bats, such as this big brown bat (bottom right), hide from predators.

BAT PREDATORS

Not all bats hunt, but all bats are hunted. Being nocturnal and dark-colored helps bats hide from predators. And flying makes them hard to catch. However, if a bat is caught or pulled to the ground, it has limited defenses. Bats aren't great fighters, and many can only shuffle slowly along the ground.

Who preys on bats? Raptors are big bat hunters, catching them in flight. Hawks, falcons, and eagles nab bats with their strong feet armed with sharp talons. Raptors eat their snagged bats on the go in midair. Some tropical raptors specialize in bat hunting—such as the bat hawk of Africa and the bat falcon of Central and South America. These expert bat hunters are crepuscular, or active at dawn and dusk, to better catch their favorite food. Owls are a truly nocturnal winged hunter of bats. Their excellent hearing and silent wings help owls catch bats in the night. Some bats fly less on bright full moon nights to avoid owls. This behavior is called lunar phobia, which means fear of the moon.

Lots of creatures will eat a bat given the chance. Bats have been swallowed by frogs and fish, eaten by tarantulas and centipedes, and even caught by large spiders' webs. Some earth-bound carnivores go out of their way to seek out bats when they're not flying. Predators like snakes, raccoons, and opossums hunt for bats at rest in roosts and hibernation sites. They climb trees, crawl into caves, and sneak into barns looking for bats. Housecats and feral cats also kill bats. These persistent feline hunters will even hang out on rooftops at dusk and swat bats out of the air as they leave their roosts.

An endangered Indiana bat
hangs in a Kentucky cave.

BAT-SAVING TEAM

Though bats are becoming better appreciated, they are still in trouble. Bat populations around the world are shrinking, and many bat species are threatened with extinction. The caves, forests, water sources, and habitats they depend on are disappearing in many places. Overhunting is a growing problem in many parts of the world where bats are food for people. American bats are also threatened by the increasing numbers of electricity-making windmills and a terrifying and mysterious new disease. White-nose syndrome is killing many millions of hibernating bats in North America. The new disease threatens the survival of perhaps half of all American bat species. Thankfully Merlin Tuttle's BCI has grown into a team of more than thirty scientists, educators, and support staff. There are thousands of members in sixty different countries.

Caves where endangered bats hibernate close to the public in winter to protect the bats.

America's Most Threatened

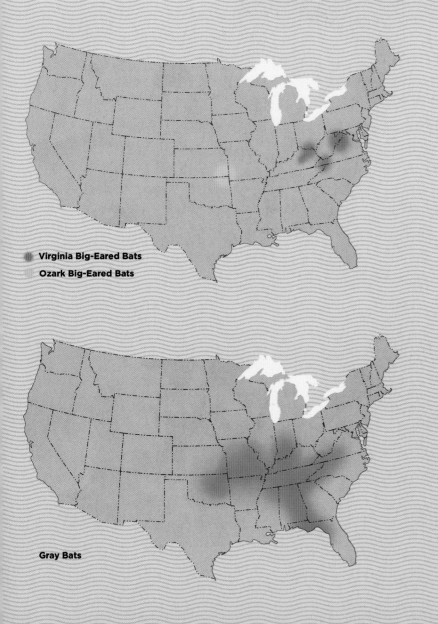

Virginia Big-Eared Bats
Ozark Big-Eared Bats

Gray Bats

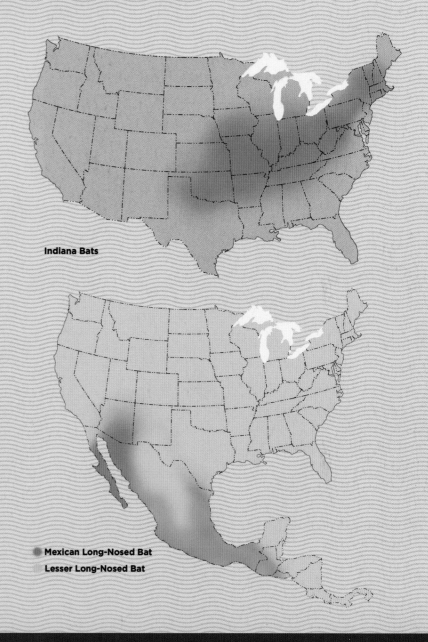

Indiana Bats

Mexican Long-Nosed Bat
Lesser Long-Nosed Bat

The six species of bats on these maps are on the U.S. endangered species list. Many more bat species are on state endangered species lists. It's likely that half of all American bat species are declining fast enough for wildlife scientists to consider listing them as either threatened or endangered, especially those affected by white-nose syndrome.

BCI's scientists and other conservationists are working around the world to help bats. They protect bat caves, support bat research, provide bat houses, and educate people about the importance and value of bats to humans and the ecosystems we share. Bracken Bat Cave is a great example of how conservation can help. BCI bought the cave where 20 million bats give birth every summer so it would be forever protected. They plan to turn the seven-hundred-acre area into a nature reserve and education center. "There is no place on the planet better suited to helping people understand and overcome their fear of bats than right here at Bracken Cave," explains Merlin. "Once you have experienced millions of bats flying right over your head, and not one single bat ever harming a human, you just can't go away with the same fear of bats."

A crowd of bat watchers thrills to the sight of millions of Mexican free-tailed bats swarming out of Bracken Bat Cave.

This young red bat
will spend its adult
life eating insects and
roosting in trees.

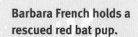

CHAPTER 2

CHANGING MINDS, RESCUING BATS

Want to see a baby bat?" asks a smiling woman with thick grayish hair. Barbara French sits in an office surrounded by bookshelves and cushioned chairs. Where could a bat be around here? Then Barbara slips a hand under her own shirt collar. That's when you notice a lump on her left shoulder under her flowery shirt. When Barbara pulls out her cupped hand, something is wriggling inside. "It's a red bat," says Barbara, opening her hand. Hanging from her fingers by teeny feet is a tiny orange-ish bat. The walnut-size baby is covered in fur the color of red hair. Bright eyes like black glass beads peer out from a big fluffy head. The youngster unfolds a small wing while opening its jaws in a yawn. "Are you getting a good stretch?" Barbara asks the bat. When she closes her hand into a cup, the bat scoots backwards, snuggling into her palm.

Barbara French holds a rescued red bat pup.

Barbara holds a rescued Mexican free-tailed bat.

questions come from curious kids. "I've been asked, 'Do bats have bellybuttons?' and 'Can bats burp?'" says Barbara with a laugh. (The answers are yes and probably, for the record.)

BUSTING BAT MYTHS

Education is the front line of bat conservation. "The single biggest threat to bats is human ignorance about them," says Merlin Tuttle. "Most people are very happy to protect bats if only they understand them." Teaching the truth about bats often means changing what people think they know. There are a lot of untrue myths about bats. (See Batty Myths sidebar, page 38.) Many people still wrongly believe that bats are people-chasing, disease-spreading vermin. A good part of BCI's bat myth–busting work has to do with the disease-spreading part. Rabies is bats' biggest image problem in North America. Many bats are killed and bat caves destroyed because of the false belief that most bats have the disease and will attack people.

Rabies is a virus that infects mammals. In the United States, bites from wildlife such as raccoons, skunks, foxes, and bats sometimes cause rabies infections. Merlin says that the risk of getting rabies from a bat is often greatly exaggerated. "Less than a half of one percent of bats contract rabies," explains Merlin. Bats don't have rabies any more than

Barbara French is a big fan of bats—a very knowledgeable fan. "BCI gets a lot of calls and e-mails from people asking all kinds of things to do with bats," says the bat biologist. She answered hundreds of messages every month as the science officer at Bat Conservation International for fifteen years. What do people want to know? Everything from how to get bats out of their homes to questions about what bats eat, how they fly, and where they live. Barbara says often some of the toughest many other wild animals, and bats rarely bite people. BCI works to clear up the misunderstanding, talking to public health people about bats and bat rabies. "Anyone bitten by a wild animal—including a bat—should be checked for rabies," says Barbara. But it's also important that people understand how valuable bats are and why they need protection.

Bats became Barbara's passion after she moved to Texas nearly three decades ago. Austin is the headquarters for BCI. It's also home to millions of bats. Barbara still remembers the first time she saw thousands of Mexican free-tailed bats flying out from under a bridge in Austin at dusk. "I was so surprised and excited! It was the most captivating sight I had ever seen," recalls Barbara. "I have been fascinated with bats ever since." That fascination led to Barbara's current job rescuing and rehabilitating bats. Like other wildlife rehabilitators, Barbara cares for injured and orphaned animals. She's given thousands of rescued bats a second chance.

MEET THE BATS

"Are you hungry, cutie?" Barbara coos. She gently holds the baby red bat as it slurps milk from a plastic eyedropper. The small bat's eyes begin to close as it drinks. Soon its stomach is full of milk. Barbara carefully puts the sleepy baby bat into a padded denim pouch.

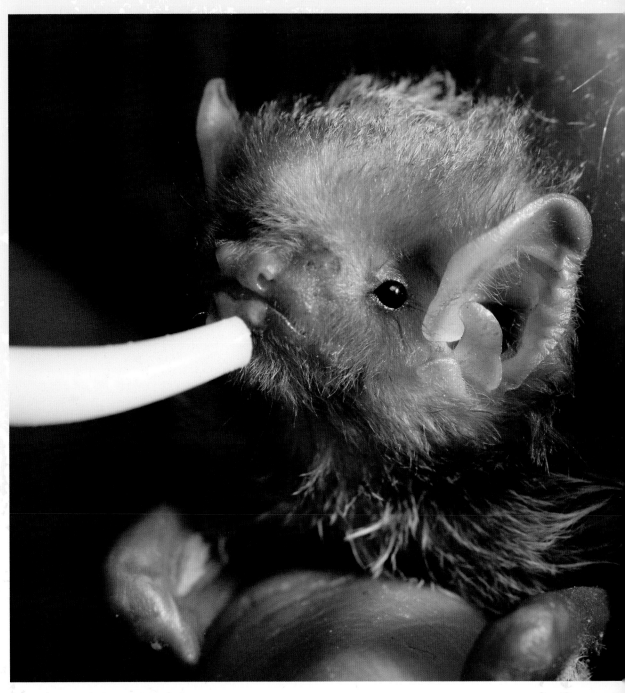

Barbara feeds milk to a rescued baby red bat.

Yellow bats, such as this one, roost alone in palm tree leaves. They are rge bats with long wings.

Big free-tailed bats are larger and blacker and have bigger ears than Mexican free-tailed bats.

Mexican free-tailed bats such as this one live in large groups called colonies.

Evening bats are common in the southern United States. They leave their roosts early in the evening, a habit that earns them their name.

The soft, hand-sewn pouches are the perfect place for young or injured bats to snuggle into. Caring for injured and orphaned bats is round-the-clock work. The bats have to be fed and cared for 24/7. Thankfully the bats live in a barn right next to Barbara's house. "I don't just do bats as my job—I also do bats as my personal life!" says Barbara with a laugh.

Barbara opens a small wood and wire cage, and gently sets the baby-bat-filled pouch inside. Similar pouch-filled cages line the walls inside the dark barn. "Who else would you like to meet?" asks Barbara. She cares for a half-dozen or so different kinds of bats, including orphaned red bat babies, injured Mexican free-tailed bats, recuperating evening bats and yellow bats, captive straw-colored fruit bats, and an elderly cave bat. They're representatives of just a few of the world's thousand-plus bat species. Bats live on every continent except Antarctica. They come in all sizes—from as small as a hummingbird to as big as an owl. More than one-fifth of all five thousand or so mammal species are bats.

The wing membranes of a bat make up about 85 percent of its body's surface area.

Flight is what makes bats unique. They became the only truly flying mammal more than 50 million years ago. The secret is their wings. Bat wings are made of naked skin over a framework of bones—the same bones we have. Barbara gently unfolds the wing of a Mexican free-tailed bat. "There's her elbow and her wrist," says Barbara as she touches the bones visible through the wing's thin skin. "And her thumb," she continues, pointing to the small nub halfway down the top of the wing. Bats are master fliers. Their flapping wings propel them forward with speed and maneuver them around trees, after insects, and into crevices.

Same Bones, Different Sizes

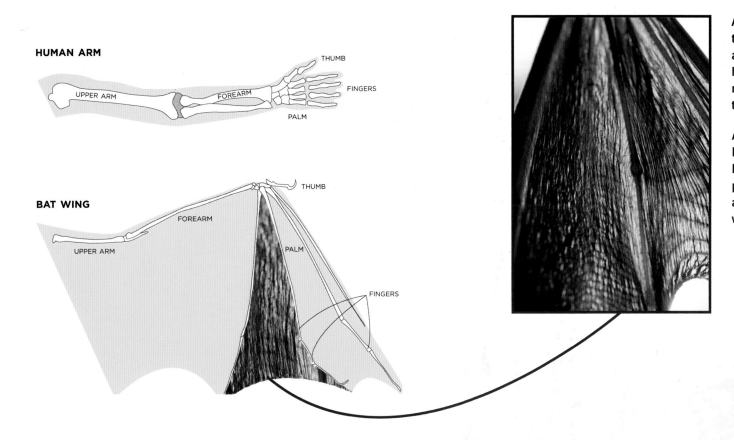

HUMAN ARM

UPPER ARM

FOREARM

THUMB

FINGERS

PALM

BAT WING

FOREARM

THUMB

UPPER ARM

PALM

FINGERS

A bat's wing is made of the same bones as your arm and hand. A bat's hand and finger bones are much longer and support the wing membrane.

A bat's wing membrane helps regulate the bat's body temperature, blood pressure, water balance, and gas exchange—as well as enables flight.

When a bat can't fly, it's in trouble. Many of Barbara's bat patients have broken or hurt wings. "The wing injuries can often be treated," says Barbara. She sometimes does bat surgery, putting pins in the broken bones. "Finger injuries will heal well, but the upper arm is much harder," says Barbara. Only bats that can fly and catch insects on their own are released back into the wild. Outside the bat barn is a big flight cage where recuperating bats exercise and can catch bugs. When—and if—they can feed themselves, Barbara releases them back into the wild. Those that can't make it on their own become bat ambassadors, traveling with Barbara to events that teach people the truth about bats.

This Egyptian fruit bat roosts in large colonies.

LIVING ON BAT TIME

Bats are unique among mammals in other ways besides flight. In general, the bigger the mammal, the longer it lives. An elephant might live seventy years, a dog fifteen years, or a hamster only two years. Bats break this rule. Even small bats can live forty or more years. For their size, bats are the longest-lived mammals on earth. Bats also reproduce slowly for their size. A mouse might have dozens of babies per year. Most kinds of bats give birth only once a year to a single pup. "One lost bat baby is a lost generation," says Barbara.

While the bat babies get milk, most adults in the bat barn eat live mealworms. "They're live beetle larvae," says Barbara. "I order eighty

This Malayan flying fox lives in Southeast Asia, where it eats mostly fruit.

thousand mealworms a month." Most North American bats are insect-eaters. They have mouths full of sharp teeth to quickly crunch up insects as they fly. Each of the 1,100 different kinds of bats is especially adapted to the particular food it eats. Fruit-eating bats have big eyes and powerful noses to see and smell the ripe tropical fruit available year round. Nectar-eating bats also live in warm places with year-round flowers. They have long noses and tongues to reach deep into flowers and slurp up nectar. There are bats that snag fish with their strong-clawed feet, bats that catch birds in midair, and even bats that ambush mice on the ground! The infamous vampire bats of Central and South America drink the blood of mammals and birds.

Most bats do their eating at night. They are nocturnal animals. So how do bats manage to fly around and find their food in the dark? Many fruit-eating bats have extra-big eyes, just like other nocturnal creatures. The African straw-colored fruit bats that Barbara cares for have dog-like faces—the reason these kinds of bats are often called flying foxes. "They depend on their eyesight and sense of smell to find fruit," explains Barbara.

Insect-eating bats are different. "Hearing is most important for them," says Barbara. "They can also smell and see, but echolocation is the biggest part of finding their food." These bats get around and hunt in the dark by "seeing" with sound.

A red bat pup licks its mother's face.

Echolocation: Seeing with Sound

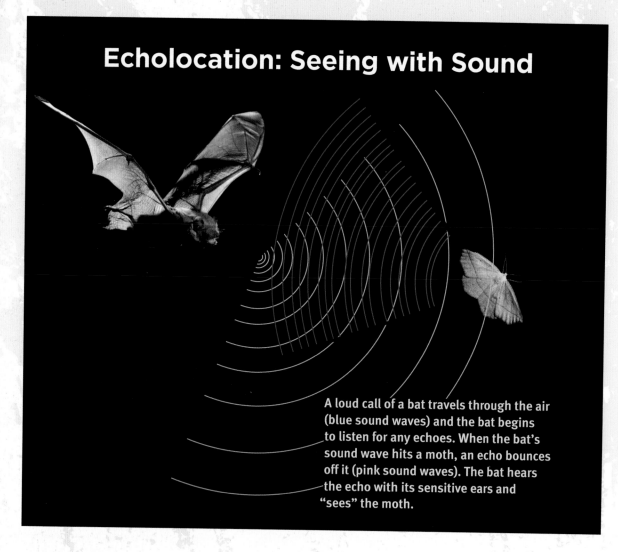

A loud call of a bat travels through the air (blue sound waves) and the bat begins to listen for any echoes. When the bat's sound wave hits a moth, an echo bounces off it (pink sound waves). The bat hears the echo with its sensitive ears and "sees" the moth.

FAR LEFT: Bat ears can detect sounds far above a human's range of hearing.

LEFT: This California leaf-nosed bat has a spear-shaped noseleaf.

A BAT'S SIXTH SENSE

Echolocation means locating something with echoes. Like sonar, it's a way to get information about something by bouncing sounds off it. Echolocating bats make loud calls and then listen for the echoes. The reflected sounds carry information about distance, speed, density, and size. A bat's brain turns the information into a kind of picture that helps the night-flying bat avoid trees, zero in on prey, and speed through caves. An echolocating bat "sees" its surroundings—caves, telephone poles, other bats, birds, and its prey—with sound. Bat echolocation is so precise that a bat can find a moth, tell how big it is, and know in which direction and at what speed it's moving, all in complete darkness. And it gathers all this information quickly enough to catch the moth while flying through a forest.

"It's why echolocators have such large ears," explains Barbara. Their big, sensitive ears collect the echoes like tiny satellite dishes. The strange faces of many bats are also echolocation tools. Those wrinkly lips and ears, leaf-shaped snouts called noseleafs, and bumpy foreheads focus the calls and echoes. Some bats even shout their calls through their megaphone-like nose. Bats are the loudest flying animals around! Their short calls or shouts are as loud as a smoke detector. Luckily for us, those echolocation calls are ultrasonic—too high pitched for humans to hear. So what is all the plainly heard chatter about inside Barbara's bat barn? "They're communicating," explains Barbara. Besides using ultrasonic calls to echolocate, bats use audible chirps, trills, buzzes, clicks, and purrs to talk to one another.

BAT CHAT

What do bats talk about? The normal stuff—food, friends, mates, territory, and complaints. The most talkative bats seem to be those that live in big colonies. Think of the mother bat coming home to Bracken Bat Cave after a night of hunting bugs. How does she find her pup among the millions of bats? One way she zeros in on her baby is by calling to it, and then the pup calls back to her. Barbara and other scientists have identified more than twenty different calls in Mexican free-tailed bats. Many were first discovered from studying the recorded conversations among the colony of fifty or so free-tailed bats in Barbara's barn. "They may even use a sort of grammar," says Barbara. "They put all of these little clicks and buzzes and trills together in certain ways to make certain meanings."

The fact that bats communicate with a complex language adds to what scientists are learning about these marvelous and misunderstood mammals. Though many people once scorned them as flying vermin, we now know that bats are intelligent, social, long-

Mexican free-tailed bats live in huge colonies of thousands and sometimes millions of individuals.

BATTY MYTHS

People still believe all kinds of crazy things about bats. Here are six of the most commonly misunderstood bat facts.

- **BATS ARE NOT BLIND.** All bats have eyes and can see quite well.

- **MOST BATS DO NOT HAVE RABIES.** Like any wild animal, bats should not be touched, especially one found on the ground, which is more likely to be sick. However, getting rabies from a bat is very rare.

- **BATS DO NOT GET TANGLED IN PEOPLE'S HAIR.** Bats are too good at flying for that—plus they generally avoid humans.

- **BATS DO NOT SUCK BLOOD.** Not even the three species of vampire bats that live in Central and South America suck blood. They lap it up with their tiny tongues. No vampire bats live in the United States, except in zoos.

- **BATS ARE NOT FLYING MICE.** DNA evidence shows that bats are not closely related to rodents. Some scientists believe they are more like primitive primates.

- **BATS ARE NOT PESTS IN NEED OF EXTERMINATION.** Bats can be safely removed from an attic or home without harming them. Bats are important pest controllers, often eating their own weight in pest insects every night.

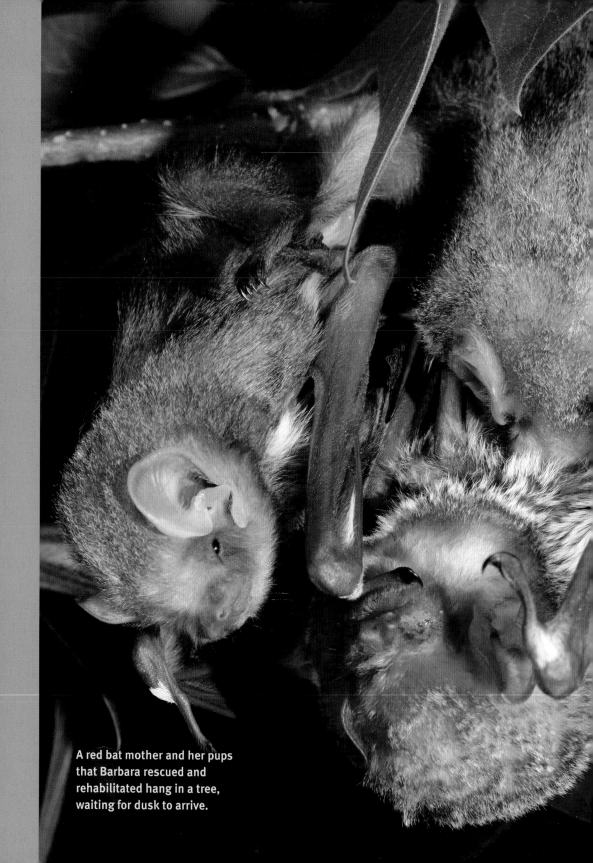

A red bat mother and her pups that Barbara rescued and rehabilitated hang in a tree, waiting for dusk to arrive.

lived creatures more closely related to monkeys than mice. And no matter where they live or what they eat, each bat species plays an important role in its ecosystem. Bats are important controllers of insects. Fruit bats pollinate plants and spread seeds that grow forests. Cave-dwelling bats and the guano they make support hundreds of unique cave species of insects, fungi, and bacteria found no where else.

Barbara stands outside near a hackberry tree. Its branches bend in the hot summer wind. Hanging between some leaves is a mother red bat. Three babies cling to her, purring as they nurse and nuzzle. Red bats are one of the few bat species that have more than one pup at a time. All that extra weight makes it hard for a mom to get back up into a tree if a windy storm blows her to the ground. "Someone found her in their yard with the babies," explains Barbara. That's how the family of four ended up at her bat barn. "I let the mom keep taking care of the babies and just fattened the mom up," says Barbara. Once she'd eaten mealworms for a few days and gotten rehydrated, the mom red bat was good to go. That's when Barbara put them onto this tree branch. The family sleeps away the afternoon in the tree. Once evening comes, the mom will fly away, carrying her babies with her. They'll have gotten their second chance.

Millions of Mexican free-tailed bats swirl and whirl out of Bracken Bat Cave every night during the summer.

Jim Kennedy identifies a
bat in Saltpeter Cave.

CHAPTER 3

GOING UNDERGROUND

You'd never know it was a hot, muggy June afternoon. It's chilly inside Saltpeter Cave. White puffs of breath come out of Jim Kennedy's mouth as he steps down into the cave. Above ground is busy Carter Caves State Resort Park in northeast Kentucky. Up top, birds sing, visitors shout, and cars buzz by. But down in the cave it's as still and quiet as an abandoned cellar. The only sounds are feet crunching on gritty rock.

An endangered Indiana bat takes flight in Saltpeter Cave.

There aren't many bats in the caves this time of year. Bats mostly use these caves for winter hibernation. As Jim leads the cave explorers, or cavers, through a tunnel and around a corner, only a couple of bats go flapping by. They're probably using the cave as a day roost—a safe place to sleep away the day. One bat hangs alone on a cave wall. "That could be an Indiana bat," says Jim, slipping on a glove.

This tri-colored bat is hibernating away the winter in a Kentucky cave. Water from the damp cave air has condensed onto its fur in pearly drops.

He carefully plucks the small bat off its rocky roost for a closer look. Indiana bats are an endangered species. Tens of millions of the dark brown insect-eating bats once lived in North America. Indiana bat populations began shrinking as settlers moved in and made many caves unusable to bats. It's no coincidence that most of America's endangered bats are species that depend on caves. Their caves are in trouble.

ROOSTS, NURSERIES, AND HIBERNACULA

All bats need shelter from the weather and predators. Bats aren't well armed for defense. Their legs and long-toed feet are adapted to hanging upside down, not fighting. Roosting in hard-to-reach places keeps bats safer from snakes, raccoons, cats, and other predators. Trees, crevices in rocks, barns, and other bat abodes also shelter them from extreme temperatures, rain, and wind. The more than a thousand kinds of bats around the world roost in all sorts of places. They sandwich themselves under tree bark, wedge into rock crevices, hang in clumps of leaves, and nestle under roof eaves.

North American bats roost in lots of different places, too, but many use caves. More than half of the forty-six species of bats in the United States spend part of their lives in caves. Some, like the bats at Bracken Bat Cave in Texas, give birth and raise pups

in caves. Many bats use caves as safe, dry day roosts. Other bats use caves as a rest stop while migrating through, or as a night roost—a resting place while foraging for food.

A big reason many of America's bats need caves is for hibernation. Cold temperatures kill off insects, leaving most American bats without food during the winter. Some bats head to warmer places to find bugs, including Bracken Bat Cave's Mexican free-tailed bats. "Most of them migrate to Mexico for the winter," says Merlin Tuttle. But many American bats hibernate during the cold, insect-free months, waking up when the bugs are back in spring.

Bat hibernation is extreme energy conservation. A hibernating bat's breathing and beating heart slow down to the minimum level needed to keep it alive. The heart of a flying bat will beat one thousand times a minute, says Barbara French. "In hibernation you can get a heart rate of ten beats per minute." A hibernating bat needs to make its stored fat last until spring. Caves are good hibernation places—called hibernacula— because they keep bats evenly cool and steadily deep asleep during the winter. That's the recipe for saving the most energy. Bats that get too warm or wake up too often waste their stored fat. "They're going to starve and not make it through the winter," explains Barbara. Without the energy-saving conditions inside caves, many bats simply wouldn't survive until spring.

These tri-colored bats are hibernating in a Kentucky cave. The tri-colored bat used to be called the eastern pipistrelle.

BAT CAVE BASICS

No one understands how important caves are to bats better than Jim Kennedy. "I run the caves program for Bat Conservation International," explains the biologist. "My passion is the cave environment and the proper management of caves." The passion part is pretty obvious by Jim's bat T-shirt, bat stud earring, bat money clip, and other batty accessories. "I've been studying bats for more than twenty years," says Jim. Some scientists become interested in bats through their study of mammals or the ecosystems where bats live. Jim's path to bats was different. "I was a caver that got interested in bats," he explains.

So what makes a cave good for bats? It depends on the bat and what it needs. A bat just looking for a place to rest for a few hours isn't very picky. Any cave will do. A summer colony of mother-to-be bats is choosier. Their cave needs to be warm—or able to be made warm with bat body heat. Bracken

RIGHT: Jim Kennedy measures the temperature outside a Kentucky cave so he can later compare it to temperatures inside the cave. FAR UPPER RIGHT: He gets his cave survey gear ready before entering the cave for the first time. FAR LOWER RIGHT: Jim collects data on hibernating big brown bats inside the cave.

Bat Cave is a good summer maternity site because it's warm and also big with a wide entrance and has "rough surfaces that the babies' feet can cling on to," explains Merlin. Bats seeking a place to hibernate during winter need different cave conditions. Winter hibernation caves need cold—but not freezing—temperatures.

The chillier the cave, the better, explains Jim: "If the bats can lower their body temperature more, they are burning fat slower." The slower the bats burn their stored fat, the more likely it will last until spring. Good bat hibernation caves stay at the same cold temperature all winter long. Up and down changing temperatures force bats to burn more fat to adjust. Caves that trap cold air are the best at creating the stable, evenly cold temperatures hibernating bats like.

PROTECTING BAT CAVES

People make trouble for caves, especially bat caves. Good bat caves are rare to begin with. Only around 5 percent of all U.S. caves have the right temperature and water conditions to be suitable for bats. People have already made many of those bat-unfriendly. Mammoth Cave National Park is a good example. "As many as twenty million Indiana bats once hibernated there before European settlement," says Jim. Two hundred years of mining, tourists, and

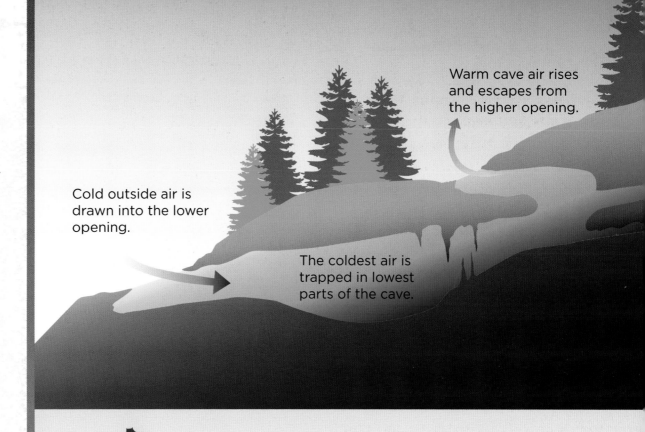

Warm cave air rises and escapes from the higher opening.

Cold outside air is drawn into the lower opening.

The coldest air is trapped in lowest parts of the cave.

HOW A CAVE TRAPS COLD AIR

Cold air–trapping caves come in a couple of shapes. Often they are caves that slope downward from their single entrance, or caves with more than one opening to the outside. When one opening is lower than the other, cold air gets trapped inside the cave during cold weather. "In the winter the cave air is warmer than the outside air," explains Jim. Cold air sinks and hot air rises. So the warmer cave air rises up and flows out of the higher opening, like smoke through a chimney. This pulls in cold outside air through the lower opening. The cold air sinks into the lowest parts of the cave and is trapped.

underground construction has made many parts of Mammoth Cave unlivable for bats. Today there are fewer than 400,000 Indiana bats left in the world. That is about the number of people who tour Mammoth Cave each year.

Bats abandon many caves because of human activities. Every year, people enter caves and kill bats on purpose. But less brutal actions can also make a cave unusable for bats. Caves have long been used as trash dumps, mined for minerals, or closed off for people's safety. Turning a cave into a tourist attraction with lights isn't good for the bats either. And because one bat colony can have millions of members, losing one good bat cave can doom countless bats. Even experienced cavers can harm hibernating bats without realizing it. It can take twenty minutes for a hibernating bat to wake up enough to move. A scout troop can be out of the cave and back at camp by the time a bat wakes up. Coming out of hibernation costs the bat precious fat. "A bat uses thirty to sixty days of stored energy to wake up," says Merlin. "That's why it's so important not to disturb hibernating bats," explains Barbara.

Cave gates like the one BCI is helping put up at Laurel Cave (see pages 48–49) make a difference. A cave gate stops people—but not bats—from entering a cave. Most modern cave gates are made of thick slats of spaced horizontal metal. The gates usually have a few

A large tour group walks up the stairs built inside Mammoth Cave in Kentucky. About 355,000 people tour the cave each year.

This Townsend's big-eared bat is hibernating in a New Mexico lava tube cave.

Most bat gates have a few removable locked-on slats so people can enter the cave when it's safe for the bats.

removable slats or a lockable door so people can explore the cave when it's safe for the bats. But when the bats need the cave—whether for winter hibernation or summer maternity time—people can be locked out. One of the most successful cave gates is also one of the largest. In 1970 Merlin Tuttle discovered 250,000 endangered gray bats living deep inside Hubbard's Cave in Tennessee. The amazing find was part of the scientist's decades-long study of the same fascinating gray bats he first encountered as a teenager.

Ninety-five percent of all the world's gray bats hibernate in only nine caves. Hubbard's Cave is one of them. By the time the giant thirty-five-foot-wide cave gate could be built in 1985, less than a third of Hubbard's Cave's gray bat population remained. Gating all three cave entrances has done wonders for the gray bats. In 2006 more than a half million bats were estimated to be living inside Hubbard's Cave. Gating a cave isn't always enough to bring bats back, however. Sometimes a cave needs restoring.

Big brown bats roost in a Kentucky cave. Big brown bats are big eaters, consuming their own weight in insects every night.

GATING LAUREL CAVE

Jim Kennedy is leaning over a pile of steel with a welding torch. Sparks shower down onto his boots as he cuts the metal. Workers wearing hardhats and headlamps heave heavy metal bars up onto their shoulders. A man in mud-covered overalls yells instructions into a walkie-talkie. It may look like a construction site, but this is Laurel Cave. Laurel Cave is one of the caves at Carter Caves State Resort Park that bats hibernate in, including endangered Indiana bats. Sadly, in 2007 more than one hundred of Laurel Cave's Indiana bats were killed. Someone entered the cave and "just purposely killed the bats," said Jim. They knocked the hibernating bats down, stomped on them, crushed them, and left others to drown on the watery cave floor.

Killing an endangered species is a crime, but these criminals were never caught. "We had a five-thousand-dollar reward fund," said Jim. But they didn't get "a single tip on who those culprits were." To keep it from ever happening again, Laurel Cave is getting gated. Cave gating isn't easy work. Heavy metal has to be cut and dragged into wet, muddy, dark places, and welded together. Every single opening to a cave has to be gated, not just the main entrance. The hard work is worth it to protect the bats. As one of the volunteer workers promised, "There's not going to be any more bat killing in this cave." Once the gates are all up, bats will easily fly between the metal slats over Laurel Cave's entrances, but human troublemakers will be kept out.

A sign in Laurel Cave warns cavers that endangered Indiana bats roost in the cave and that it is illegal to enter during hibernation season. Laurel Cave is in northeast Kentucky's Carter Caves State Resort Park.

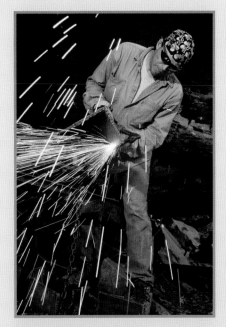

Jim cuts steel bars for the bat gate near the entrance to Laurel Cave.

The bat gate bars must be buried deeply so no one can dig under them.

Jim carries a steel slat for the Laurel Cave bat gate.

Each steel slat of the bat gate is spaced to leave room for bats—but not people—to pass through.

Every entrance to a cave must be gated for a bat gate to work.

Each steel slat is welded into place on the gate.

A volunteer welder finishes up the gate over this narrow entrance of Laurel Cave.

FIXING WHAT'S BROKE

"We can fix caves," says Jim. He means caves that people have altered and made unsuitable for bats. He's driving a screw into a low ceiling back inside Saltpeter Cave. Rock grains rain down loudly onto the floor in the quiet cave. The screw anchors a small plastic thing that looks somewhat like a mini smoke detector. "It's a data logger," explains Jim. The device collects temperature and humidity information inside the cave every few hours for months. Bat scientists use the data loggers to find out what conditions are like inside caves. Studying a cave's conditions helps conservationists know what it needs to be more bat friendly. The data loggers also let scientists track the conditions over time so they can tell if what they're doing is making a cave better for bats.

Long ago Saltpeter Cave was popular with bats. "It might have had 100,000 bats," says Jim. Evidence of past bats remains on some ceiling areas and walls of Saltpeter Cave.

It's called roost stain. "Roost stains are the brownish stains left behind by the bats from their body oils on their fur and skin," explains Jim. Roost stains sort of look like patches of rusty smudge on the cave ceiling. Along with bat bones and old guano, roost stains give clues to how many bats once lived in a cave. Bat scientists can even use roost stain to estimate past bat numbers. "It's not one hundred percent accurate," says Jim, but it can tell you whether a cave only had a few bats, or lots of bats.

Jim Kennedy attaches a data logger to a cave wall in Saltpeter Cave. This data logger will record temperature and humidity levels inside a cave, mine, bat house, or other roost over many months.

Jim stands in the open air dam in Saltpeter Cave. The door is closed in the winter to help trap cold air in the cave.

Most of Saltpeter Cave's bats left when people took over the cave, digging out a mineral to make gunpowder in the 1800s and later opening it to tourists. "This cave has been disturbed for two hundred years," says Jim. Proof of bothersome people is everywhere— lights and electric wires hang from the ceiling, graffiti is scratched and scrawled on rocks, and the floor is a dugout flat walkway. Less obvious is the cave's temperature and humidity. It's a bit warm and too dry for many hibernating bats. Humidity is important in a cave. Like all animals, bats lose moisture through their mouth and nose while breathing. If a cave's air is too dry, the bats get dehydrated and die while hibernating.

Saltpeter Cave is dry because not much fresh outside air gets very far back into the cave. Why not? Some of its small sinkhole openings were filled in with trash years ago. This plugged up the cave and kept moist air from flowing through it. BCI is working with Carter Caves State Resort Park to restore the cave to its once more bat-friendly condition. In the summer of 2008 workers dug out a sinkhole so more air could get through. Volunteer cavers also built an air dam for one of the passageways. It looks like a door with a slot in it that the bats can fly through. "The air dam slows down the airflow and forces it into some of the side passages," explains Jim. That way the cold winter air swirls into corners, sinks, and gets trapped in the cave, making it cooler.

An endangered Indiana bat roosts on old graffiti on the wall of Saltpeter Cave. People have been disturbing the cave for two centuries.

Once the right conditions have been restored to a cave, bats will return to it. Bats are constantly checking out new caves and other possible roosts. "If you build it, they will come," jokes Jim. The cave restoration work at Saltpeter is proof. "We went from about thirty Indiana bats up to almost seven thousand," says Jim. "That's been very, very encouraging." And making a cave suitable for bats isn't just good for the bats. Bats are good for caves, too. "By protecting the habitat of bats, you're saving all kinds of things in caves," explains Jim. Cave creatures such as salamanders, insects, fish, and crayfish depend on bat guano to fuel and fertilize the very unique ecosystems inside caves. "Bats are an umbrella species," says Jim. Their protection also safeguards other living things. Helping bats survive helps many other species survive, too.

Mylea Bayless watches a bat fly away after examining it under a highway bridge.

CHAPTER 4

BUILDING BAT HOMES

A woman gently holds a brownish bat with a gloved hand. A bat-print bandanna covers her head, but not much of her long hair. "He's got to be at least three weeks old," says Mylea Bayless. The young bat is furry, not a hairless newborn pup. The scientist carefully puts the bat back up into its roost. Mylea has to speak loudly over all the noise—the traffic noise. The scientist is crouched under a busy interstate highway bridge in central Texas. Semi-trucks, SUVs, and cars thunder overhead at seventy miles per hour. The site may be a concrete and steel jungle, but it's home to more than a million Mexican free-tailed bats.

As dusk arrives, bats leave the bridge where they spent the day roosting in gaps underneath the roadbed.

In this series of images, Mylea uses a flashlight to look at bats under a Texas highway bridge. The maternity colony of Mexican free-tailed bats are roosting in the gaps under the roadbed. Mylea catches some of the bats in a net, then she examines one.

These big brown bat mothers and pups are roosting under an Ohio bridge.

Mylea shines a flashlight up underneath the bridge. The bottom of the bridge is made of giant slabs of concrete laid side by side, like slats on a wooden bench. In between the concrete slabs are dark gaps that go all the way up to the roadbed. When Mylea focuses the flashlight on one of the gaps, something moves. "Do you see the babies?" she asks. Wedged up in the inch-or-so-wide gaps are mom and baby bats. This bridge shelters a maternity colony. "One of the things I think is kind of cool about bridges is that they're like a permanent bat house," says Mylea.

More than a million Mexican free-tailed bats leave their bridge roost as the day ends.

FAKE ROOSTS FOR REAL PROBLEMS

You've probably seen bat houses. They often look a bit like wide, flat birdhouses. People hang bat houses on their homes, and often parks put them up on poles to attract bats. Bats use the boxes as roosts, places to safely sleep away the day or raise pups. Gardeners like bats because they eat pest insects and mosquitoes. Some bat fans just like to watch the bats fly out in the evening. Bat houses help people connect with bats and educate them about bat benefits. But bat houses and other human-made, or artificial, roosts also help bats survive.

Bat populations are dwindling all over the world. "One of the most frequent causes of their decline is loss of natural roosts," says Merlin Tuttle. Caves aren't the only natural roosts getting harder for bats to find. Many American bats roost in old trees for much of the year. They spend summer days snoozing under loose bark or raising pups inside woodpecker-drilled holes. "Bats use the trees that are rotten and falling apart," explains Mylea. "Because that's where you get cracks and crevices, and sloughing bark and cavities." Unfortunately old, dead, and dying trees are not popular with many people. Landscapers cut them down so they don't fall on buildings. And trees grown for lumber are harvested

The bats in this bat house eat lots of harmful pest insects in this Texas pecan grove.

A row of bat houses welcome bats in a Pennsylvania field.

This old barn has been home to generations of big brown bats in southwest Ohio.

long before old age. When much of America's forests were first cut a hundred or more years ago, some of the bats moved into abandoned barns, buildings, wells, and mines. Now even these "unnatural roosts" are disappearing. They're being torn down and filled in for safety reasons or to make room for new homes, highways, and factories.

Bats need three things—food, water, and roosts. Two out of three won't do, explains Mylea. "If food and water is available but we've taken out all the big trees, they've got no place to roost." This can happen when a forest is divided up, or fragmented. Good wildlife habitat might still be there, but now farms, homes, or roadways separate it into chunks. Mylea says that bat houses can provide homes across fragmented landscapes. They can give bats a place to roost where there's food and water. Artificial roosts can also provide needed rest stops as a bat travels between food-filled habitats or migrates to its hibernation cave.

Mother big brown bats and their pups roost in the rafters of a barn.

HELPING HOMELESS BATS

Helping roostless bats is Mylea Bayless's job. She's the artificial roost specialist at Bat Conservation International. Mylea was raised around wildlife. Her father was a park ranger. "I was kind of a tomboy," she admits. "I grew up hunting and fishing and running around in the woods with my dad." Her love of the outdoors led to a career in wildlife biology, and eventually BCI.

Part of Mylea's job is heading up BCI's bat house program. It educates people on how and where to put up good bat houses. (Interested in putting up your own bat house? See page 78 to get started.) After fifteen years of studying different shapes, sizes, colors, designs, and placements of bat houses, BCI knows what works. Mylea says they've got it right "because ninety percent of bat houses built and installed correctly are being used by bats." The key to a good bat house is crevice size. "Most American bats like to live in crevices just three-quarters of an inch wide—the space that best protects them from predators," explains Merlin. Bat houses that provide the right size spaces work best. Even when those crevices are underneath a busy bridge.

Mylea Bayless carries her bat-catching equipment toward a bridge where bats roost.

This row of bat houses is behind a Pennsylvania school.

Different bat species happily share this large bat house.

A little brown bat snuggles into a bat house's wooden crevice. Little brown bats are very common in the northern United States. Females will often return to the same maternity roost year after year.

CELEBRITY BRIDGE BATS

It's just a Wednesday afternoon, but there's a festive feeling in the air. Families are gathering on a grassy hill in the middle of a city. Kids and dogs run through a sprinkler as adults unfold lawn chairs and pull snacks out of bags. A teenager wanders through the crowd selling glow-in-the-dark toys. The grassy hill full of people is beside a lake where a bridge ends. As evening approaches, tourists gather on top of the bridge, too. They lean on the railing and look out over the water. Everyone is waiting for the bats to come out.

This is Congress Avenue Bridge in downtown Austin, Texas. Underneath the bridge that leads to the state capitol building is the largest urban bat colony in North America. "For some twenty-five years an estimated one and a half million Mexican free-tailed bats have lived in bat-house-like crevices beneath this bridge," says Merlin. The bats started showing up after engineers rebuilt the bridge in 1980 using concrete slabs that unknowingly created bat-size crevices. After thousands of bats moved in, local health officials wrongly said that the bats were rabid and dangerous. People began signing petitions to have the bridge bats exterminated.

Merlin Tuttle and BCI soon came to their defense, telling Texans the truth about bats. Not only were the bats nothing to fear, Merlin

A spotty cloud of Mexican free-tailed bats fly out from under Congress Avenue Bridge.

Every summer evening in downtown Austin, Texas, bat watchers gather near the famous bridge.

said, but they were something to be grateful for. The Mexican free-tails living under the bridge eat tens of thousands of pounds of pest insects every single night! The city eventually embraced the bats. "No one has been harmed and the people of Austin now love their bats," says Merlin. And the bats do put on quite a summer-night show. Every year more than 100,000 tourists from around the world spend some $11 million in Austin to see the bats.

As the sun lowers in the sky, a breeze picks up. The air flowing under the bridge carries a musky guano smell to the bat watchers on the grassy hill. Then it happens. Flocks of flapping, chattering bats start to stream out from under one end of the bridge. They dip down and then zoom up in a twisting column. Soon a river of living, flying bats stretches all along the lake bank and off into the distance as far as you can see. And the bats just keep coming, pouring out from under the bridge for a half hour or so.

Bridges like Congress Avenue have become important roost sites for many bats. More than half of the forty-six species of bats in the United States roost in bridges and other road structures such as culverts. As states and cities learn about the benefits of pest-controlling, tourist-attracting bats, others are building bridges with bat-size crevices or adding large bat houses underneath existing bridges. Many towns now want their own bat bridge!

ABOVE: Mexican free-tailed bats dot the sky above downtown buildings in Austin, Texas.

LEFT: Bat watchers on Congress Avenue Bridge get a close-up look at departing Mexican free-tailed bats.

STAND-INS FOR HOLLOW TREES

Though many bats roost in bridges and bat houses, some bats aren't fans of squeezing into crevices. "There are two species of bats in the southeastern United States that typically live in big hollow trees," says Mylea. Rafinesque's big-eared bats and southeastern (myotis) bats raise pups inside huge hundred-year-old hollow trees. These bats hang upside down in the roomy rotted-out trees with insides as smooth as a wooden barrel. "Old-growth hollow trees are probably one of the most rapidly disappearing roost types anywhere," says the wildlife biologist. There isn't much centuries-old uncut forest left in North America. Hurricanes, storms, and decay are toppling the ones that remain. And although these bats will also roost in caves or abandoned buildings, few will use traditional crevice-filled bat houses.

Losing roost sites is taking a toll on these hollow-tree-loving bats. Both Rafinesque's big-eared bats and southeastern bats are listed as either threatened or endangered in every state they live in. These rare homeless bats

BCI scientist Michael Baker (left) and National Park Service biologist Steven Thomas (right) get ready to install a data logger into one of the roost towers built for Rafinesque's big-eared bats at Mammoth Cave National Park in Kentucky.

need a different kind of artificial roost. "We're working on designing towers that basically mimic a hollow tree," explains Mylea. "The towers are fourteen feet high and about four feet wide." They're made of regular concrete building blocks—easy to buy and haul out into the woods. BCI has helped parks and wildlife agencies build more than twenty towers. They've put them up in areas where hurricanes have knocked down lots of old hollow trees and where old buildings with bats in them are collapsing or being torn down.

"We're seeing a lot of success with the towers," says Mylea. "Bats have been slowly moving in." Rafinesque's big-eared bats

have already given birth in roost towers in Mississippi and east Texas. Mylea is also studying the temperature differences inside the towers to improve their design. The wildlife biologist says that though the towers help homeless bats, they aren't really a permanent replacement for roosts. "You don't want a whole forest full of concrete artificial trees," Mylea says. The towers are hopefully just a temporary home. "The bats have a place to live while the forest recovers over the next hundred years." The same could be said for all artificial roosts. "In a perfect world we wouldn't even need bat houses, because they'd have plenty of places to roost without them."

Rafinesque's big-eared bats roost in an artificial roost tower.

MINES FOR BATS

Most bat houses and other artificial roosts can't provide the cold, stable temperatures of a hibernation cave. One human-made structure that can is a mine. Abandoned mines have long been used by bats forced out of caves. Then in the 1990s governments started requiring old mines to be closed up so people couldn't enter them and get hurt. "And in the early days of those closures, literally millions of American bats got buried alive," says Merlin. BCI quickly began to work with the mining companies to save the bat colonies. "We showed them that we could build bat-friendly gates that would also protect people," explains Merlin. The gates are often cheaper than bulldozing a mine shut or capping every entrance with concrete. Thousands of old mines across North America are now important bat sanctuaries. "Literally millions, perhaps a majority, of remaining American cave-dwelling bats now live in abandoned mines," says Merlin. "The mines are kind of arks of last refuge."

Pennsylvania Game Commission wildlife biologist Cal Butchkoski measures the air temperature outside a bat gate covering abandoned Hartman mine that is now a winter hibernation site for more than 22,000 bats.

Bat gates on mines, like those on caves, can be unlocked and opened so people can enter.

ABOVE: A group of bat experts heads down to tour Hartman mine. The steep rocky slope was bulldozed under the entrance on purpose. It helps trap sinking cold air down inside the mine during the winter, which is why 22,000 bats choose to hibernate there.

LEFT: Six different species of bats hibernate in the mine, including endangered Indiana bats. The mine is one of Pennsylvania's largest bat hibernacula.

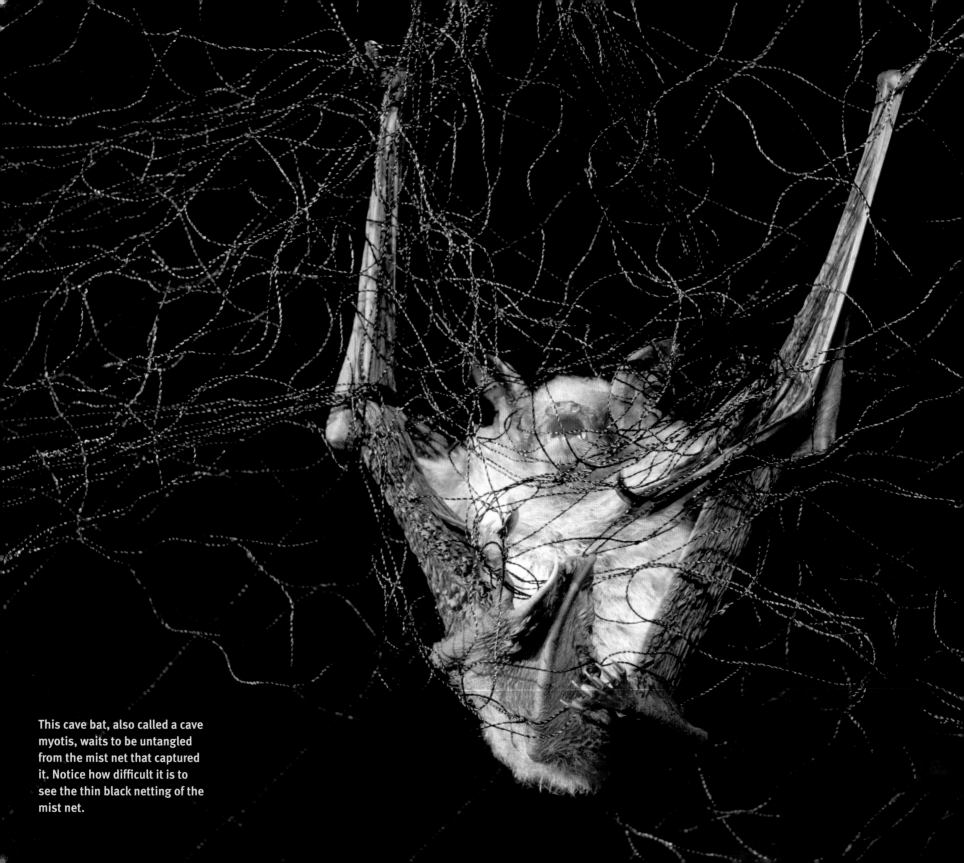

This cave bat, also called a cave myotis, waits to be untangled from the mist net that captured it. Notice how difficult it is to see the thin black netting of the mist net.

CHAPTER 5

DISCOVERING BATS' SECRETS

After sleeping away most of the day, Elizabeth Braun de Torrez is working through the night. Studying bats sometimes means living on bat time. The ecologist walks through a pitch-dark pecan orchard. Elizabeth, or Liz for short, stops next to something nearly invisible. It's a high, wide wall of thin black netting—a mist net. The thirty-foot-tall bat-trapping net is hung between two poles among the pecan trees. Liz's headlamp shines brightly on a tangled ball of net and fur—a bat. She works quickly to free the sparrow-size bat, which squeaks out complaints. Liz untangles the bat's claws from the net threads. She holds it firmly but gently with one gloved hand while keeping her ungloved fingers away from the bat's teeth. Once it is out of the net, Liz slips the bat into a small cloth bag. "It's a cave bat, *Myotis velifer*," she says, pulling the bag's drawstrings.

Once released, the cave bat will go back to hunting small moths and beetles.

A ranger at Mammoth Cave National Park in western Kentucky educates visitors about white-nose syndrome. Before entering the park's caves, visitors are asked to disinfect their shoes if they've been in other caves within areas infected with the fungus.

She knows the bat's species and its scientific name, but Liz wants to learn more. "There's a lot unknown about bats," says the scientist. Everything from why bats live so long to how they evolved is uncertain. Even where some North American bats migrate, look for food, or roost throughout the year remains a mystery. "Bats are the least studied of all mammals," says Merlin Tuttle. "The opportunities for new discoveries are just wide open." Though discovery is exciting for scientists, not knowing many bat basics can make their conservation difficult. How can you help a bat if you aren't exactly sure how its body functions, what it eats, or where it lives year round? It's like working in the dark—without a headlamp.

THE GREAT WHITE PLAGUE

Understanding bats better has never been more important. There's a new mysterious problem killing bats in eastern North America. White-nose syndrome (WNS) affects bats during their winter hibernation. Its name comes from a white fungus that grows on the faces and wings of affected bats. WNS causes bats to wake too often, so they burn up their stored fat and starve long before spring. Many die inside their hibernation caves or mines. Others wake up starving and fly out in the middle of winter—and even in daylight—in a desperate search of food. Thousands of bats are being found dead and dying in the snow outside caves and mines. Some caves and mines are so severely stricken with WNS that bat carcasses carpet the entire cave floor.

More than six million bats have died from WNS since it was first discovered in 2006 in a New York cave. It's now spread throughout New England, into Canada, as far south as

The muzzle of this little brown bat is covered with white-nose fungus. Scientists photographed the bat in a cave in New York in the fall of 2008.

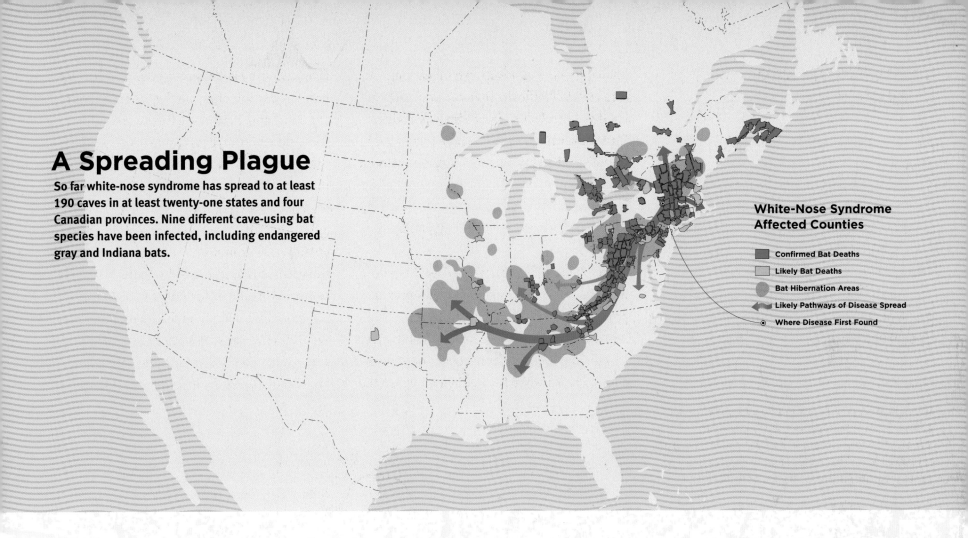

A Spreading Plague

So far white-nose syndrome has spread to at least 190 caves in at least twenty-one states and four Canadian provinces. Nine different cave-using bat species have been infected, including endangered gray and Indiana bats.

White-Nose Syndrome Affected Counties

- Confirmed Bat Deaths
- Likely Bat Deaths
- Bat Hibernation Areas
- Likely Pathways of Disease Spread
- Where Disease First Found

Alabama, and as far west as Oklahoma. At this rate, the disease could sweep across the whole country within a few years. So far WNS has infected nine species of insect-eating bats in regions east of the Rocky Mountains. But half of the forty-six U.S. bat species hibernate or roost in caves. So at least two dozen kinds of American bats are potentially at risk from the fast-spreading disease. Unfortunately, among the infected are endangered Indiana bats, gray bats, and Virginia big-eared bats. These species' most important remaining hibernation caves are now threatened. Up to 100 percent of bats may die in a WNS-infested hibernacula.

When the dangerous bat disease was first discovered, Merlin Tuttle and BCI, along with bat researchers at universities and state and federal wildlife agencies, scrambled to find some answers about WNS. "I've studied bats for fifty years and have headed up BCI's worldwide conservation efforts for twenty-seven years," Merlin Tuttle told the U.S. Congress in 2009. "Never in my wildest imagination had I dreamed of anything that could pose this serious a threat to America's bats." At the time, no one was yet sure what exactly caused the disease, how it spread, and why it harmed bats. As we come up on a decade into the bat plague, more is known about the WNS fungus and the bat disease it causes. Unfortunately, this knowledge hasn't helped sick bats. Treating a disease in wildlife is not as easy as giving a dog, cat, or horse a pill.

TRACKING DOWN A KILLER, QUARANTINING CAVES

Scientists now know with certainty what causes white-nose syndrome. It's called *Geomyces destrucans,* a cold-loving, cave-dwelling white fungus that sickens bats. The fungus infects their skin, chewing holes in their wings and covering their muzzles and ears with sores. Bats infected with the WNS fungus aren't able to hibernate normally. They awake too often, become dehydrated, use up their stored fat, and die before spring comes.

The WNS fungus isn't a new species, just new to North America. After *Geomyces destrucans* was identified as WNS's cause, scientists went looking for it elsewhere. "They went around to several sites in Europe, took fungal swabs, and grew them on

White-nose fungus spores could be catching rides from cave to cave on the muddy clothes or gear of cavers like this one.

cultures," says Katie Gillies. She heads up Bat Conservation International's efforts to understand and battle white-nose syndrome. When scientists checked the genetic makeup of the European fungi, they found the same fungus that's killing American bats. *Geomyces destrucans* doesn't seem to cause WNS in Europe. Perhaps it's been in the caves there long enough for Europe's bats to adapt to it. Diseases often do the most damage to new populations. "That is why North American bats are so vulnerable to infection," explains Katie.

No one knows for sure how *Geomyces destrucans* got here. Maybe the white-nose syndrome fungus hitched a ride to America on a traveler's shoe or backpack. Scientists believe the fungus spreads mostly from one bat to another. But cavers might be speeding the spread by accident. When a person walks into a cave, fungus spores can easily stick to the visitor's clothes, boots, or other gear. Those spores—and the fungus that sprouts from them—can then be spread to other caves that the caver later visits.

Thousands of people a year used to visit the New York cave where WNS was first identified. Now it is closed to prevent visitors from possibly spreading the bat disease to other caves. The U.S. Fish and Wildlife Service has closed caves and abandoned mines on federal lands and is asking cavers to stay out of caves with bat hibernacula in states with WNS. Hundreds of caves are now closed, including

Laurel Cave and Saltpeter Cave, featured on pages 41–51. For now they are open only to the remaining bats. No one is sure when it will be safe to reopen them to human explorers.

Tracking down the killer fungus was a big step. But it hasn't yet resulted in any sort of cure for bats. There are chemicals that kill fungi. "But you can't spray fungicide in a cave without altering the ecosystem," explains Katie. Caves are full of all kinds of fungi, most of which are important to the unique wildlife that live in caves. Trapping and treating individual bats isn't practical either. Researchers are still looking for possible solutions.

So what's going to happen? As things stand right now, we're going to see a big die-off of bats, says Katie. With nothing to stop it, WNS will burn through cave-dwelling bat populations across the continent. "It's probably not going to kill every single bat on the landscape," she says. "We do see some survivors." The species of bats that aren't infected by WNS will make up a bigger percentage of future bat populations. Those individual bats that survive or are immune to WNS will hopefully give birth to offspring resistant to the fungus over time. It will take time, however, because bats reproduce very slowly. "It will be many, many, many generations before they're able to recover," says Katie. Bats will recover, she says. "But not in our lifetimes."

A healthy tri-colored bat hibernates in a Kentucky cave. It's one of the most common species of bats in eastern North America.

A little brown bat (bottom) and a tri-colored bat (top) hibernate together in a Kentucky cave. Both are among the nine species of bats with WNS.

CLEANABLE CAVES

Bellamy Cave in Tennessee is the winter hibernating site of 270,000 endangered gray bats. When white-nose syndrome showed up in the cave, the Nature Conservancy decided to try something different. In 2012 they built an artificial cave. The concrete cave is near the entrance to Bellamy Cave, so conservationists hope that some gray bats will find it and try hibernating there. Recorded bat calls will be played in the fall to attract bats to the fake cave's opening. Inside the artificial cave are cameras and temperature sensors to help scientists study the bats. Once spring comes and the concrete cave is empty, workers will scrub it clean of any fungus—something you can't do in a real cave. A fungus-free place to hibernate will hopefully slow down the spread of WNS in Bellamy Cave and among gray bats. If bats take to it, abandoned mines and other constructed caves could be similarly made suitable for hibernating bats.

The artificial cave is like a giant concrete box: eighty feet long, sixteen feet wide, eleven feet high, and buried under four feet of dirt. (Photo © Cory Holiday/The Nature Conservancy)

NATURAL PEST CONTROL

Back in the Texas hill country, where WNS is not yet a problem, Liz is doing what she can to find out more about the bats in this pecan orchard. "I'm an environmentalist at heart, as well as a scientist. My passion is trying to help conserve natural areas, wild areas," says Liz. She believes that orchards, ranches, and farms can both grow food for people and provide habitat for wildlife—like bats. Liz hopes that more orchard owners will want to help bats if her research shows how bats can help them. Putting up bat houses and providing good bat habitat such as old pecan trees are ways they can keep bats around. Bats are important insect controllers for farmers. Nut-eating insects are a big problem, especially the

ABOVE: Liz Braun de Torrez collects bat guano from cups that sit under a bat house. She'll send the guano to a laboratory that can identify the insect species eaten by the bats from the insect DNA in the guano.

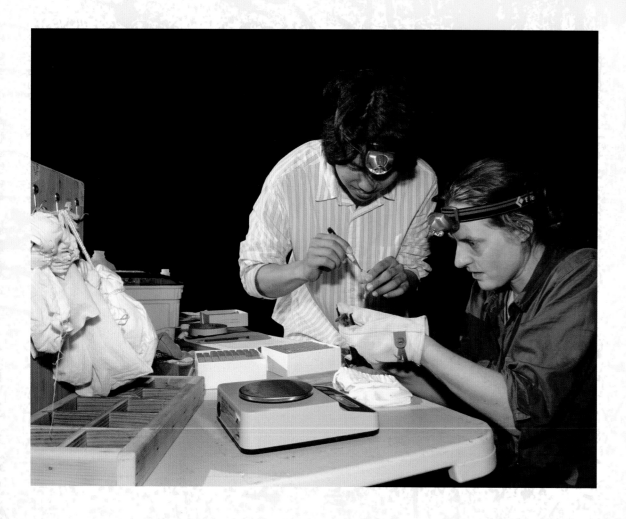

LEFT: Liz and her assistant study their captured cave bat in the middle of a dark pecan orchard around midnight.

pecan nut case-bearer moth. "One adult can lay between fifty and one hundred and fifty eggs," says Liz. Each individual egg is laid on a young pecan nut, which is ruined when the larva hatches out and eats a hole in it.

"We want to know if the bats are eating any pecan tree pests," Liz explains. And if so, which species of bats are eating the pecan pests. To find out, she's brought the captured bats over to a folding table set up in the dark orchard. The table is crowded with clipboards, calipers, tweezers, a laptop computer, and other equipment. With a gloved hand, Liz carefully coaxes the caught cave bat out of its bag. Inside the bag is some bat droppings, or guano. "This is the important part," says Liz. "We collect guano to see what they're eating." The guano is put into a little plastic vial and labeled. A laboratory can identify the insect species from DNA in the insect leftovers in the guano. With its guano safely stored, the cave bat is measured and weighed. Liz writes down its sex and age, too. "It's a juvenile male," she says.

The next step is giving the bat a wing band, a tiny metal clip that looks a bit like an ear cuff. On it is an identification symbol made up of letters and numbers. She slips it over the bat's largest wing bone—the forearm—and squeezes it on. "We put the bands on so when they're hanging upside down you can read the symbol," explains

Liz finishes putting a wing band onto the cave bat's forearm.

Liz. That way a caver or other bat researcher can easily write it down. Last up is taking a bit of wing skin. "It heals up in a couple of weeks," Liz promises as she punches a small hole in the bat's wing. The skin gives her a DNA sample for the bat. If it's ever caught again, scientists will be able to tell how much it's grown, how old it is, whether it's eating something different, and where it came from.

Bat wing bands are engraved with unique identification codes made up of letters and numbers.

KILLER WIND

Wind energy is a great way to make electricity without polluting. Unfortunately, the giant spinning blades of electricity-making windmills, or wind-energy turbines, are deadly to bats. Wind turbines kill tens of thousands of North American bats every year. "One study showed that just sixty-four turbines killed two thousand bats in six weeks," says Merlin Tuttle. "That's a serious cause for concern." Especially since thousands of new wind turbines are going up every year.

Scientists aren't completely sure how wind turbines kill bats. Many of the dead bats found at wind farms show no injuries. Rather than being struck by the turbines, many bats appear to be killed by a sudden drop in air pressure near the spinning blades. Like those of a scuba diver coming up too fast, the tiny blood vessels inside the bats' delicate lungs explode.

Scientists have discovered that most bats are killed during periods of low wind during the late summer or fall. BCI recently found that by simply not spinning turbine blades during periods of low wind, 70 percent of bat kills can be prevented. The amount of electricity sacrificed to save bats is very little. "It's a loss of less than 1 percent of energy production," says Merlin.

BCI is also encouraging wind energy companies to choose turbine sites that are outside of bat migration pathways. It's not just a problem for wind farmers. These migrating bats are headed to ecosystems across North America. A bat killed by a wind turbine will never eat the pests in the cornfield it was migrating to.

Wind energy turbines make electricity without polluting, but can be deadly to bats.

LISTENING AND SEEING IN THE DARK

Having done its part for science, the cave bat leaps off Liz's open hand. He flaps off into the black night. Researchers get a lot of information from bats like these, but they can capture only a few a night. Thankfully technology can also help scientists know what kinds of—and how many—bats are flying around without netting them. One tool is a thermal imaging camera. Liz sets up the special camera near a big bat house just before dusk. "The camera measures heat," she explains. It records images of the bats coming in and out of the bat house. Each one shows up as a little spot of heat compared to the cooler dark night sky in the background. A computer program counts each bat "hot spot," something nearly impossible for humans to do. Counting thousands or millions of bats is not easy! Thermal imaging cameras let bat scientists get real numbers, not just estimates, of how many bats are living in a bat box, cave, or other roost. Another tool researchers sometimes use to see bats in the dark are night-vision scopes or goggles, like the ones soldiers use in night battles.

When it comes to studying bats, often listening is easier than looking. Scientists have been using technology to eavesdrop on bats for many years. Bat detectors are devices that turn a bat's ultrasonic echolocation calls

Liz Braun de Torrez takes video of bats leaving a bat house with a thermal imaging camera. A computer program will count each bat on the video, telling Liz how many bats are using the bat house.

These bats flying out of a bat house at night are difficult to see—and count.

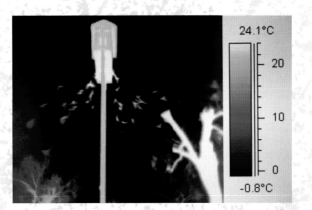

The thermal imaging camera makes a color-coded video using heat. This picture from the video shows bats flying out of the bat house.

Bat scientists glued the small red lightstick onto the back of this big brown bat. (The gloved hand is holding it.) When the bat is released, the scientists will use the bat-detecting instruments to follow the bat and record its calls. The lightstick will later fall off.

Merlin Tuttle uses a bat detector to listen to bats at Bracken Bat Cave near San Antonio, Texas.

into sounds humans can hear. If you've ever been on a guided night hike, the park ranger likely brought along a bat detector. It makes a static-like sound as bats fly overhead. Bat researchers use sophisticated bat listening devices that can record and analyze hours of bat sounds. Different devices can be programmed to count individual bat voices, identify bat species by sound pattern and frequency, and record bat behaviors such as feeding or flying through an area. Liz sets up bat call recorders in the orchards where she nets bats. The recordings help her know if the bats are feeding in the orchards—or just flying through. Once the recordings are downloaded into a computer, the program graphs the sounds it recorded overnight into a sonogram. The echolocation calls of bats just flying through look different from those hunting. "You can see the feeding buzzes on the sonogram," explains Liz. These are the fast bursts of sound a hunting bat makes to zero in on its found prey.

Figuring out where bats are going takes different technology. Bat researchers track bats in a number of ways. The same kind of weather radar that tracks storms can also show where large groups of bats go to find bugs. The huge colonies of Mexican free-tailed bats in Bracken Bat Cave and under Austin's bridges show up as clouds of color on central Texas radar. "Doppler weather radar shows

Merlin stands in front of a poster of the 2002 U.S. postage stamps that featured some of his amazing bat photographs.

that they often go almost directly to croplands, where they predominantly feed on armyworm and corn earworm moths, which are billion-dollar crop pests in America," says Merlin. Following a migrating bat is a bit tougher. Using radio telemetry, scientists can track bats during their migration from hibernation cave to summer roosts. The researchers capture bats and glue a tiny temporary radio microtransmitter on each bat's back. Then researchers use antennas to follow the bats. It's not easy work. Bats are small and easy to lose while you're driving around at night, following a weak radio signal from a tiny microtransmitter that eventually falls off or quits working when the tiny battery is used up. Bat tracking isn't for quitters, but then, neither is bat conservation.

Merlin Tuttle watches Mexican free-tailed bats fly out of Bracken Bat Cave, one of his favorite sights.

No one knows this better than Merlin Tuttle. He's proud of all that BCI has accomplished in the fight to save bats, but he's worried. "It is also alarming to see how much is yet to be done and how little time there is to do it if we are going to make a real difference," he says.

"We can't just help the most popular animals and save ecosystems," explains Merlin. Bats play an important role in so many ecosystems. They eat insects, pollinate plants, and spread seeds. Whether you like bats or not, the plants and animals of many ecosystems depend on them. "And when we allow ecosystems to be endangered, we endanger our own future." Bats' survival is tied to our own. By saving bats, we're protecting ecosystems of all sorts. As Merlin says, "Life on this planet would not be the same without bats."

LEARN MORE ABOUT BATS

Websites
- Bat Conservation International: www.batcon.org
- Bats 4 Kids: www.bats4kids.org
- How Stuff Works (Bats): animals.howstuffworks.com/mammals/bat.htm

Books

America's Neighborhood Bats: Understanding and Learning to Live in Harmony with Them by Merlin D. Tuttle (University of Texas Press, 2005)

Bats in Question: The Smithsonian Answer Book by Don E. Wilson (Smithsonian, 1997)

Do Bats Drink Blood? Fascinating Answers to Questions About Bats by Barbara A. Schmidt French and Carol A. Butler (Rutgers University Press, 2009)

Stokes Beginner's Guide to Bats by Kim Williams (Little, Brown, 2002)

How to Help Bats
- Buying this book will help bats. A portion of the royalties from this book will be donated to Bat Conservation International (www.batcon.org).
- Put up a bat house. Find out how at www.batcon.org (click on Get Involved and then Install a Bat House).
- Adopt a bat or support your local bat shelter. Learn more at www.batworld.org (click on Adopt a Bat! and Local Rescue).

- Make your yard more inviting to bats by not using pesticides and by planting native night-blooming flowers that attract insects bats like to eat, such as moonflower, cornflower, common four-o'clock, phlox, and salvia.
- Be a friend to bats by leaving them alone where they roost and staying out of bat caves during hibernation. If a bat gets in your house, open doors and windows so it can escape instead of calling an exterminator.

White-Nose Syndrome

As this version of the book goes to press in early 2013, WNS continues to spread across the United States and into Canada. Scientists, conservationists, and wildlife agencies continue to study the disease and ways to possibly fight it. Unfortunately, many more millions of bats are being infected every year. The future of North American cave-hibernating bats remains uncertain.

Here are some websites that will give you the latest news on the battle against WNS:
- whitenosesyndrome.org
- www.batcon.org/WNS
- www.fort.usgs.gov/WNS

WORDS TO KNOW

biologist—a scientist who studies living things.

calipers—an instrument used to measure thickness, diameter, or length of a small object.

caver—a person who explores or studies caves.

colony—a group of animals in a particular place of the same species.

conservationists—people who preserve, manage, and care for the environment.

day roost—a place for bats to sleep away the day.

DNA (*deoxyribonucleic acid*)—the substance in genes that passes on the characteristics of living organisms.

echolocation—the radar-like way that bats (and other animals including whales) translate their own sounds and echoes into a map of their surroundings to navigate and find food.

ecologist—a scientist who studies the relationships between living things and their environment.

ecosystem—a system made up of a group of living things, their environment, and the relationships between them.

endangered—in danger of becoming extinct.

extinct—died out; no longer existing or living.

guano—the solid waste of bats.

habitat—the place where an animal or plant naturally lives.

hibernaculum—a place where an animal hibernates.

hibernation—a period of time when an animal is inactive and its energy conserved by lowering its body temperature, slowing its breathing, and using little fat.

insectivore—an insect-eating animal.

mammal—a warm-blooded animal with fur or hair that gives birth to live young that nurse mother's milk.

maternity colony—a group of mother animals and their young of the same species in a particular place.

migrate—to move from one region to another when the seasons change.

myotis—a group, called a genus, which includes about eighty-five different small insect-eating bats including the cave bat, Indiana bat, southeastern bat, gray bat, little brown bat, and small-footed bat.

night roost—a temporary resting place for bats while foraging for food at night.

nocturnal—active at night.

noseleaf—the fleshy flap on the front of the nose of some bats.

primate—group of mammals that includes humans, apes, monkeys, and lemurs.

population—a group of organisms of the same species living in the same place.

rodent—group of small mammals, including mice, rats, and squirrels, that have sharp front teeth used for gnawing.

roost—a place for bats to sleep or rest; to settle in for sleep or rest.

roost stain—brownish stains on cave walls and ceilings left behind by the bats.

saltpeter—naturally occurring potassium nitrate, a white mineral used in making gunpowder, in preserving meat, and in medicine.

scrub—arid landscapes of pines, oak, bushes, and tough grasses.

sinkhole—a depression in the surface of the land created by a cave roof collapsing underneath it.

sonogram—a graph or image created with sound vibrations.

species—a category of living things made up of related individuals able to produce offspring that can themselves reproduce.

telemetry—a technology that allows for remote measurement and reporting of information.

threatened—not currently endangered but still threatened with extinction or likely to be endangered in the near future.

tragus—the bump of skin in front of the opening to a bat's ear.

ultrasonic—sounds with too high a frequency to be heard by the human ear.

INDEX

Page numbers in bold type refer to photographs and their captions.

Australian ghost bat, **11**

Baker, Michael, 62
Bat Conservation International (BCI)
    on bat deaths from wind turbines, 74
    bat house program, 58
    cave protection, 24, 46
    cave restoration, 51
    caves program, 44
    founding of, 16
    mission, 24
    myth-busting work, 28
    roost tower construction, 63
    work with mining companies, 64
    worldwide membership, 22
bats
    benefits to humans, 10, 72–73
    body parts, **9**
    diet of, 11, 34
    facts about, 8
    geographic distribution, **11**, 31
    to help and learn more about, 78
    myths about, 28, 38
    role in ecosystem, 10, 39, 77
    vocabulary terms concerning, 79
    wing structure, 32, **32**, **33**
Bayless, Mylea
    on importance of roosts, 57
    job with Bat Conservation International, 58
    study of bats under highway bridge, **52**, 53–55, **54**, **55**, 58
    on tree-roosting bats, 62, 63
BCI. *See* Bat Conservation International (BCI)
big brown bat, **11**, **47**, **54**, 57, **76**
big free-tailed bat, **31**
Bracken Bat Cave
    emergence of bats from, 19, **19**, **39**, 77
    entrance, **18**
    environment in, 14–15, 44–45
    Mexican free-tailed bats in, **12**, 13–14, 15
    protection of, 24
Braun de Torrez, Elizabeth "Liz," 67–68, **72**, 72–73, **73**, **75**, 75–76
Butchkoski, Cal, **64**

California leaf-nosed bat, **36**
cave bat (cave myotis), **66**, **67**
caves
    bat gates, 46–48, **47**, **49**
    conditions favorable to bats, 43–45, **45**, 51
    data collection in, 50, **50**
    human destruction of bat-friendly environment, 16, 28, 45–46, **46**, 50, 51
    white-nose fungus in, 68, **68**, 70, **70**
communication among bats, 37

echolocation
    ears and other physical features for, 36, **36**
    human detection of, 75–76
    "seeing" with, 34, 36, **36**
    ultrasonic calls, 36–37
Egyptian fruit bat, 34

Egyptian fur bat, **11**
endangered bats in America, **23**
endangerment of bat populations
    human activity in caves, 16, 28, 45–46, **46**, 50, 51
    human predators, 16, 48
    loss of roosts, 56–57, 62
    variety of threats, 22
    white-nose syndrome, **68**, 68–71, **69**
    wind turbines, 74, **74**
evening bat, **31**

flying foxes, 11, 34
French, Barbara
    care of injured and orphaned bats, 27, **27**, **28**, **29**, 29–31, 33, 39
    on echolocation, 34, 36
    on energy conservation during hibernation, 43, 46
    identification of bat calls, 37
    job with Bat Conservation International, 28, 33
    on rabies, 29

gates, 46–48, **47**, **49**, 64, **64**
gray bat, 15–16, **16**, **23**, 47
greater horseshoe bat, **11**

hibernation
    in caves, 43, 45
    dehydration, 51
    energy conservation, 43, 46
    hibernating bats, **16**, **42**, 43, **47**, **71**
    infection with white-nose fungus, 68
Hubbard's Cave, 47

Indiana bat
    in abandoned mine, **65**
    as endangered species, **22**, **23**, 41, 43, 46
    habitat destruction, 45–46, 51, **51**
    human attack on, 48
instruments for data collection, 44, 50, **50**, **75**, 75–76, **76**

Kennedy, Jim
    bat identification, **40**
    cave data collection, 44, 50, **50**
    gating of Laurel Cave, 48, **49**
    job with Bat Conservation International, 44
    repair of damaged caves, 50, 51
    on temperature of hibernation caves, 45

Laurel Cave, 46, 48, **49**, 70
lesser long-nosed bat, **17**, **23**
little brown bat, **59**, 68, **71**

Malayan flying fox, **11**, **34**
Mammoth Cave National Park, 45–46, **46**
Mexican free-tailed bat
    in Bracken Bat Cave, **12**, 13–14, **14**
    calls, 37
    emergence from cave, 19, **19**, **24–25**, **39**, 77
    formation of colonies, **31**, 37
    physical features, 13, **13**
    predators, 19, **20**, **21**
    roost under highway bridge, 53, **54**, **55**, **60**, 60–61, **61**

winter migration, 43
Mexican long-nosed bat, **23**

National Zoo, Washington, D.C., 71

Old World fruit bat, 11
Ozark big-eared bat, **23**

predators of bats, 16, 19, **20**, **21**, 43, 48

rabies, 28–29, 38
Rafinesque's big-eared bat, 62–63, **63**
red bat, **26**, **27**, **29**, **35**, **38**, **39**
roosts. *See also* caves
    abandoned mines, 64, **64**, **65**
    barns, **57**
    bat houses, 56, **56**, 57, **58**, **59**
    bats' need for, 43, 57
    highway bridges, **53**, 53–55, **54**, **55**, **60**, 60–61, **61**
    loss of natural roosts, 56–57, 62
    towers, **62**, 63
    trees, 56–57, 62

Saltpeter Cave
    closure of, to visitors, 70
    data collection in, 50, **50**
    day roost, 41
    human activity in, 51, **51**
    Indiana bat in, 41
    restoration of, 51
    temperature and humidity, 50, 51
southeastern (myotis) bat, 62
Swainson's hawk, **21**

technology for study of bats, 44, 50, **50**, **75**, 75–76, **76**
Thomas, Steven, **62**
Townsend's big-eared bat, **47**
tri-colored bat, **42**, **43**, **71**
Tuttle, Merlin
    on danger of wind turbines, 74
    founding of Bat Conservation International, 16
    on importance of bats' survival, 77
    on importance of education about bats, 28
    on lack of knowledge about bats, 68
    photography of bats, 15, **15**, 16, **19**, **76**
    protection of bats under highway bridge, 60–61
    on roosts in abandoned mines, 64
    on spread of white-nose fungus, 69, 70
    study of bats, **13**, 13–16, **16**, **47**, **76**, 77
    on worldwide loss of natural roosts, 56

vampire bat, **11**
Virginia big-eared bat, **23**, 71

white-nose syndrome (WNS)
    endangerment of bats, **16**, 22, 68, **68**, 69–71
    to learn more about, 78
    spread of, 69, **69**, **70**, 71
wind turbines, 74, **74**
wings of bats, 32, 32–33, **33**

yellow bat, **30**